OPEN YOUR HAND

OPEN YOUR HAND

Teaching as a Jew,
Teaching as an American

ILANA M. BLUMBERG

RUTGERS UNIVERSITY PRESS

New Brunswick, Camden, and Newark, New Jersey, and London

Library of Congress Cataloging-in-Publication Data

Names: Blumberg, Ilana M., 1970- author.
Title: Open your hand : teaching as a Jew, teaching as an American /
    Ilana Blumberg.
Description: New Brunswick, New Jersey ; London : Rutgers University Press,
    [2018] | Includes bibliographical references.
Identifiers: LCCN 2018019617| ISBN 9781978800823 (hardback) |
    ISBN 9781978800816 (paperback) | ISBN 9781978800847 (mobi)
Subjects: LCSH: Blumberg, Ilana M., 1970- | Jews, American—Israel—Biography. |
    Jewish women college teachers—Israel. | Jewish women college teachers—
    United States. | Humanities—Study and teaching. | Israel—Biography. | United
    States—Biography. | BISAC: EDUCATION / Philosophy & Social Aspects. |
    BIOGRAPHY & AUTOBIOGRAPHY / Educators. | SOCIAL SCIENCE /
    Jewish Studies. | EDUCATION / Inclusive Education. | BIOGRAPHY &
    AUTOBIOGRAPHY / Religious. | RELIGION / Education.
Classification: LCC DS113.8.A4 B58 2018 | DDC 378.5694/8092 [B]—dc23 LC
record available at https://lccn.loc.gov/2018019617

A British Cataloging-in-Publication record for this book is available from the
British Library.

www.rutgersuniversitypress.org

Manufactured in the United States of America

For my father, Paul Noam Blumberg, in gratitude

CONTENTS

Note on the Text   ix

Introduction   1

1   Learning to Teach, Teaching to Learn: Kindergarten to
    College—Beit Rabban and Michigan State University   7

2   Choosing to Learn, Learning to Choose:
    "Smith" Middle School   87

3   "It's the Land": "Smith" School and Jerusalem   119

    Postscript: Shadow Schools—Kindergarten to College,
    America and Israel   159

    Discussion Questions   183
    Acknowledgments   187
    Notes   189
    Bibliography   193

NOTE ON THE TEXT

This is a work of nonfiction. I have changed the names of all parties at Michigan State University and at "Smith School," and many of the names of students at Beit Rabban. Where names remain actual or student writing appears, it is with the express permission of the people in question. Classroom sessions described here are either transcribed from notes or represented to the best of my memory. Every event described here happened.

OPEN YOUR HAND

INTRODUCTION

December 2016, Jerusalem—The sun shines high in the sky and the air is cool, but on my way home from the neighborhood café, I pause to take off my wool scarf because it is already getting warm. This is winter. Although we have been in Israel two and a half years now, I still find it entertaining that as soon as the Jewish autumnal holidays end, children begin to go to school in boots and earmuffs instead of the sandals and T-shirts they wore the week before. For those of us who know weather—my husband, my three children, and myself—this seems sweet and mildly crazy. I know that what we are looking at in this sudden shift of wardrobe is biblical, liturgical weather, not meteorological. After the holidays, we begin immediately to pray for the blessing of rain: hence, the children's boots.

I know about the boots because in the mornings at about 7:30, I am in the habit of watching the city walk to school. Very young children tend to be escorted by older siblings, an occasional parent accompanying or watching from a distance. Older kids, sixth-graders, also serve as crossing guards, wearing reflective vests and yelling, *Ptach, sgor* (open, close) to the drivers, who obey these young citizens reflexively. Children here sport big and heavy backpacks: no lockers in the elementary schools. They wear colorful T-shirts with the various school insignias. By now, I know where to go to get these ironed on.

In my south Jerusalem neighborhood, religious boys wear shorts, jeans, or sweatpants with crocheted *kippot* on their heads, girls wear skirts, always with leggings, cropped in the summer and long in the winter, so they can hang upside down on the monkey bars or turn cartwheels during recess.

From my balcony, I can see my nine-year-old son, Shai, and his friend stopping at the corner market to buy a fresh roll and chocolate milk (*shoko v'lahmania*). This is a morning treat he always asks for and I sometimes allow him.

School is our Israeli education in the most comprehensive sense: as adults, in my case and my husband Ori's; as children, in the cases of Priya (age twelve), Shai (nine), and Tzipora (seven). Learning what to pack for the mid-morning meal, deciphering new report card formulations, following the culturally incomprehensible conversations on the parents' WhatsApp group: these are our acclimation.

They are also the undeniable measure of how different we are. Many things simply do not make sense to me—that a third of the children don't show up on Fridays, for instance, or that there are three different teachers, notebooks, and class sessions for "Reading Comprehension," "Literature," and "Hebrew"—and my children both fight those things and fight me for not understanding. They say, "It's crazy." But when *I* say it's crazy, they say, "That's how it is here, *Ima* (mom)"—the implication being that if I understand how school works, I might begin to understand an entire society.

And they are not wrong. I am coming to know Israel through its educational institutions, just as I came to know the United States as a student and then a teacher. Granted, one learns only subcultures, but now from the vantage point of a different country, I see that subcultures, too, are rich and telling, if partial, indicators of host societies.

Although this story will end in Jerusalem, it is mainly an account of teaching as a Jew and an American, a perspective sharpened now by contrast. Born in Israel in 1970 to two American parents, I grew up in the United States from the age of two and was educated in its private Jewish schools and then its research universities. Over time, I became a teacher, scholar, writer, wife, and mother in the United States. From my first, formative job as a kindergarten-first–grade teacher in a tiny, innovative Jewish day school in New York City, to my decade and a half teaching in major midwestern research universities, to my volunteer hours in a failing urban public school, what I know about education I learned on American soil. It is also fair to say that much of what I know about the United States I learned in and from its schools. American, as well as Jewish, experience shaped the questions of faith and citizenship that arose from my double vocation of teaching and writing. These questions now shape this book that is being written in Israel.

This book—and a swerve in my professional trajectory—was prompted by a crisis fifteen years into my university teaching career, a dramatic moment in which college students I particularly liked prompted me to ask myself whether I was successfully transmitting anything that mattered, as I taught year after year of humanities. In a new course I had fatefully titled "Truth Telling in American Culture," I found my students pushing me to reconsider the most basic assumptions I held about my work as a teacher, a vocation I could not separate from my identity as an observant Jew and a passionate American.

Simply put, I had been teaching with the belief that there was no meaningful education, whatever the immediate content, without ethics and that the deepest purpose of teaching and studying, particularly the humanities, was not self-advancement or personal pleasure, but the transformation of a world in urgent need of intelligent, sustained care. I had believed that my students knew this about me and about our study, and that we were involved in a shared endeavor, even if only within the limited space of our classroom, over a single semester.

Yet my students did not reflect such an understanding back to me. In fact, as I will narrate later on in these pages, at the moment of my crisis, they reflected back something like the opposite. The great majority expressed no need to "give back," to share, or to consider their advantages or the disadvantages of others not represented in our classroom. They left me confronting anew my place as a person of faith in a secular academy, facing fundamental questions about my vocation. Why did I teach? Why did I teach where I taught? Whom had I taught? What had I taught?

Over time, as I recovered my equilibrium and examined the intensity of my own reactions, I refined the questions. What was the relationship I sought between teaching subject matter and skills, on the one hand, and teaching moral values, on the other hand? How might one teach values in a public institution without advocating a particular politics or faith? On the other hand, how would one *avoid* teaching values? What was my role as a teacher in shaping young citizens in a democratic United States? How was I choosing which children and youth in which to invest my time and best energy? If I were free to do so, how might I remake a teaching life—intellectually and practically—to address the pressing historical reality in which I found myself as a Jew and as an American at the turn of the twenty-first century?

These questions ushered me into a new phase in my professional life in which I found myself traveling, in memory and actuality, across the variety of classrooms whose dramas make up the bulk of this narrative. I have always tended to consider myself a teacher before a professor, in part because I have been fortunate to teach in a range of settings wider than many humanities professors traditionally encounter. I came to the world of the university after teaching young children in a fledgling Jewish school in New York City whose ambitious intellectual mission was in no way separate from its moral vision. My questions returned me now to memories of those formative experiences at Beit Rabban during the early 1990s. I unearthed photographs, one video, and many written records: from detailed accounts of class sessions I had reconstructed on the same day they had transpired to the occasional letters I had written to send home to parents; from examples of student work I had collected in my notebook of lesson plans penciled in the barest of shorthand. I reread our curriculum from those years and engaged in new conversations with the school's founder.

Even as I found myself absorbed by the past, my questions demanded new action and new research. Prompted by the class sessions that had disturbed me, I set out both to volunteer my skills and to learn the realities of public education in the poorer districts of my home state, Michigan. I found my way to what turned out to be an appallingly failed public middle school. I arrived there every other week for a few months in the winter and spring of 2012 to teach young teenagers some poetry and encourage them to write.

I traveled from that school back home to Ann Arbor, where my questions accompanied me through the rituals and improvisations of mothering my three young children with my partner, Ori. Although I continued to teach my courses at Michigan State University, the questions encouraged me to arrange for our family to travel to Israel the following year, on my sabbatical. Fourteen months later, we returned to Israel as immigrants, my husband and I bringing our American democratic ideals to this modern Jewish sovereignty. Now, in the imperfect democracy that is Israel, my questions present a new face, as I find myself teaching in university classrooms paradoxically more diverse and less segregated by race, religion, or ethnicity than any I ever encountered in the United States.

Perhaps the distinguishing feature of this book will be my travel *among* classrooms, as I pursue a unified project that became more distinct to me as I tested it across diverse settings. Simply put, I sought to help students come to see themselves, in moral relation to others, by reading and writing as a community. While this story is idiosyncratic to my own circumstances and commitments, I hope it will be meaningful to all adults who see themselves as learners and teachers—whether in their homes, their classrooms, their work or volunteer places, their houses of worship, or their recreational spaces—and who know that there is more work to do than any one of us can do alone.

1 ◆ LEARNING TO TEACH, TEACHING TO LEARN

Kindergarten to College—Beit Rabban and Michigan State University

Sometimes the courses we teach choose us. In 1996, I was a graduate student in English literature at the University of Pennsylvania with the opportunity to design my own first-year writing seminar. Although I was specializing in Victorian fiction, struggling to make sense of Trollope's church politics (what was the difference between a bishop and a deacon anyway?) and George Eliot's apostasy, and even Dickens's Christmas tales, I found myself proposing a seminar far from England and its many churches and articles of faith.

As if from nowhere, a syllabus materialized in which, with extreme clarity, I laid out a course of study that paired texts about American slavery with those on the Shoah, the Holocaust of European Jewry, to investigate the relations between literacy and historical trauma. I was compelled by stories of what seemed impossible to write but had to be written. I wondered how language could bring together realities that seemed impossible to solder: the before, during, and after of lives shaped or interrupted by extreme violence and then restored or newly established as "ordinary" lives of human dignity. How could the same language suffice to capture both realities? How could the same letter *I* represent a self who had lived a life nearly impossible to credit from the other side?

At the same time, I was fascinated then—as I remain today—by the differences between fictional and nonfictional accounts of these crises, that is, the intersections of the literary and the historical.[1] I knew the course needed to begin with autobiography. I wanted the voices of those who had been there—those who had seen and suffered because of the accidents of their birth, and then written to testify—to survive. But I wanted fiction, too—works that said you can inhabit others' experience. The accidents of your birth matter, but they can never be all that matters. In a world where they are all that matters, we may find ourselves witness to or engaged in racial slavery or ethnic cleansing.

The work of the course insisted that across time and space, we are all human beings. To meet each other, there is such a thing as research; there is such a thing as responsible historical imagination. Boundaries can be crossed. Sometimes they must be crossed—with care and extreme caution.

I could not have known it in 1996, but I would wind up teaching variations of that course to American college students for nearly twenty years, in three different universities. Every time I thought of setting it aside, another student would tell me that he or she had never read such things, that they had never considered a world organized by the wholesale abrogation of some people's human rights—that all they had known came from flat textbooks or shiny museums. And then, again, I would feel I did not have the right to stop teaching it, even when I wanted to.

Looking back, it is striking to me now that this course, with its shattering content, was from start to finish a writing course. For almost twenty years, I chose to teach students the mundane freshman skills of "reading and writing" from sacred texts of suffering and survival. These were texts that attested to the power of literacy to oppose wrong; to reassert identity and sometimes community; to describe the reverberations of history in our bodies, our families, our houses of prayer, our national institutions. Painstakingly, I taught the workaday things I had been hired to teach—close reading, topic sentences, working with quotations, building a descriptive thesis—from these texts, written in fire and blood. I married form and content: I taught the power of the word through powerful words, giving our own amateur attempt to formulate ideas the charge of historical responsibility—of world making.

I believed that teaching such texts and such skills might make actors of readers. This was my unconscious answer to the role of an educator in a world visibly roiled by war, hatred, murder, and competing, perhaps irreconcilable, needs and interests. I trusted—perhaps naively—that if you read such things, you would feel you had no alternative but to take to the streets, or to the pen, or to certain kinds of work or volunteerism because the world still held no shortage of troubles: genocide; slavery; dehumanizing labor and living conditions that made education nearly unattainable; impossible, violence-inducing gaps between haves and have-nots. I believed that reading such texts would make you seek out the injustices in what the ancient rabbis called your own *daled amot*, that is, your own near environs.

As I taught and retaught that course on American slavery and the Shoah, students and sometimes colleagues would ask me how I understood the coupling of those two bodies of material: What did it mean to set these histories next to each other? I asked myself this question, too, and when I could not articulate a satisfying theoretical answer, I returned to my practical answer: to attend intently to the particularities of each text we studied, to elucidate differences, and to note commonalities—not to compare historical wounds.

But a new clarity arrived when my seventy-five-year-old Israeli uncle, a historian who had been hidden as a child by Poles during World War II, told me, in the heat of summer in Beer-Sheva, that he could not understand how I had paired American slavery and the Shoah. It was then that I understood for the first time that what I was teaching was my own ethical identity, my deepest commitments as a Jewish American, Gen-X adult. I was teaching my rationale for a vocation in education that had come as naturally as I had grown as a girl.

My two sets of texts constituted a coherent pair for a simple reason: both insisted, implicitly or explicitly, on the inviolable nature of every human life and the consequent obligations to a legal and social system built on justice and equality. This was the still, small voice: the calm, unwavering meeting point of Jewishness and Americanness that constituted the moral logic of my universe and my teaching. I saw my students, semester after semester, as just such human beings. Their existence was sui generis; their lives were valuable and briefly laid before me for nurturance. I saw them, especially the freshmen, as my charges.

When I ask myself where this intense consciousness of the sacred and the equal began, I think of my earliest encounters as a schoolchild studying the book of Genesis. In that book, human history—not Jewish history—begins as follows: "And God created humankind in God's image." Remarkably, over the course of my childhood and adolescence, the sacred nature of God's creation of humanity seemed to lead naturally to the democratic ideals of equality and justice: if each human being is created in God's image, then we are all of equal worth, with equal rights as a consequence. This distinctively American reading sidelined many other dimensions of the biblical worldview to teach a set of ethics that made national sense.

When religious faith settles upon central national values, it charges them with spirit. For better or for worse, children brought up on this meld of religious and national values do not experience them as a set of beliefs so much as a way of being a person in the world. To this day, it is impossible to say whether I believe in democratic values as a Jew or an American. And it was and is impossible to separate my sense of self from these values.

It is worth pointing out a second commonality in my growth as a young Jew and American that is less frequently part of the contemporary discourse of identity politics: I experienced both identities as *demands* that required my response. Yes, being an American and a Jew granted me rights, and armed me with pride, but first and foremost, these identities presented me with social and spiritual obligations. This sense, too, came from my study of the Hebrew Bible, which alternated its stories of belonging with commands in the second-person singular and plural. These were imperatives: "You must"; directives: "You will"; and future perfect forms: "And when you will have."

This moral grammar was not alarming to me, nor was it especially burdensome; it was merely descriptive. As a child, I had learned the strangely fatalistic verse *Lo yehdal evion mi'kerev ha-aretz* (the poor will never cease from the midst of the land) and its corollary, "Thus I command you saying, *pato'ah tiftah et yadkha l'ahikha, la'aniyekha, u'levionkha b'artzekha* (you shall open your hand to your brother, your suffering, and your poor in your land)" (Deuteronomy 16:11). Intuitively, it was clear to me that what was being described were not static identities—I was not meant always to rescue others. I was meant to fulfill whatever role I was cast in, in a set of scenes that were to be played interchangeably by a full cast. It was obvious to me, too, in the way that things are obvious to children, that "my brother," was both male and female, Jewish and non-Jewish, American and non-American. Finally, poverty, too, was a broad category. It was not limited to economic class, but applied to need of all sorts. That verse and its practical clarity attests to the strong sense of harmony I felt between Americanness and Jewishness. As an American and as a Jew, I felt I was my brother's keeper, my sister's keeper, and that they were mine.

Yet it was impossible to deny that being a Jew often separated me from other Americans in favor of all-Jewish environments, particularly in the matter of my schooling. In fact, in spite of my looking a lot like other Americans of my age and class, and consuming the same television shows, music, magazines, and books, I had never studied with non-Jews until I reached college and university. Remarkably for a child who had grown up in the Midwest of the United States, the university was the first place I came really to *know* non-Jews. This was not the result of prejudice or xenophobia but the reality of a comprehensive Jewish education in a non-Jewish society.

I differed not only from most non-Jewish Americans but from most Jewish Americans of my class, generation, and geographical location, because my Jewish education was not incidental, secondary, or piecemeal. It was far more than a few hours of after-school, culturally inflected babysitting. Instead, my Jewish education was intensive and thoroughgoing; it extended beyond two decades and left nothing untouched.

First, it was textual: from kindergarten forward, I studied Jewish texts—literary, scriptural, liturgical—in Hebrew, for as many hours a day as I studied in English. (This meant that by the time I reached ninth grade, I was in school more than nine hours a day.) I studied ancient and modern Jewish history, and learned the Bible and its commentaries: medieval, modern, and contemporary. I studied Jewish codes of law and compilations of legend. I learned to chant the Five Books of Moses and the Prophets, and the scrolls of Esther and Song of Songs, Lamentations and Ruth, and so committed long passages from all of these to memory. I became near-fluent as a reader, writer, and speaker of modern Hebrew.

My Jewish education was not only textual and intellectual; it was also immensely material, and that near counterpart to material—spiritual. I ate only kosher food in prescribed fashions, with blessings before and after meals, and intervals between milk and meat. My daily, weekly, and yearly calendars were defined by sunsets and stars and wine that divided holy from ordinary time and dictated the nature of those times. (New shoes for Rosh

Hashanah and Passover; new dresses, too.) I prayed daily, sometimes privately, but also among friends, family, and teachers in school, summer camp, and synagogue. On holidays, my parents and siblings and I watched the American world around us proceed as usual, as we walked in our fine clothes to synagogue. Each fall, we built a sukkah in a climate not intended for outdoor eating, let alone sleeping, in September or October. We looked up at the stars through the slats and leaves decorating the roof of our temporary dwelling and considered the exodus from Egypt and the promise God had made Abraham that we would be as numerous as the stars in the sky. And we didn't trick-or-treat; we had no Christmas tree or Santa Claus; we had no Oreos (not kosher at that time); no McDonald's; no Kentucky Fried Chicken; no television on Shabbat. We had good relations with our non-Jewish neighbors, but we did not make meals together.

Neither, as I have said, did we study together. During my many years of schooling, I never attended a public American educational institution. My parents, both of whom had studied at an Orthodox Jewish day school as children—my father through middle school and my mother through high school—had chosen to send me to Jewish day schools out of inherited and personal commitments, and I never questioned this decision. In the absence of a Jewish day school in Ann Arbor, Michigan, where we lived until I was ten, they helped establish the school that would educate me (and later, coincidentally, my children) as a Jew. When we moved to Chicago, I studied at well-established Jewish schools through twelfth grade and then traveled to Israel for a year of intensive study at an institute where Jewish girls from around the world studied Torah together from morning until evening. In other words, I had studied with Australian, British, Canadian, Polish, and Israeli Jews before I studied with American non-Jews.

Alongside an intellectual and ritual life, my education trained me to help others. Mainly, I was taught to help other Jews: old Jews, sick and poor Jews, Soviet Jews, Israeli Jews. I experienced this partiality as an enactment of the rabbinic logic that the poor of "one's own city" preceded the claims of the more distant poor. If we all took care of our own, wouldn't everyone be taken care of?

But who were "my own"? What was my "city"? Was this meant as metaphor? If it were not metaphor, then why were non-Jews who lived twenty minutes away from me not receiving the attention I was giving Jews in Moscow or Israel?

These questions began to claim my attention as a young adult. As a child who packed baskets for families in need, sang for hospital patients, and demonstrated and wrote letters on behalf of the Soviet refuseniks seeking visas for religious freedom, and later as a teen who visited an old-age home every week in my free time and organized a rotation of visitors from my high school, I had my hands full. Throughout my education, I studied the complicated laws of *tzedaka* (the Hebrew word typically translated as "charity," but whose etymology traces to "justice"), deepening my understanding over the years, but mainly, I did the things that adults told me—or showed me—needed doing. (I was the granddaughter of a woman who sent back a few dollars in an envelope to every appeal for *tzedaka* that she received, without fanfare or deliberation.)

Becoming an adult meant discerning on my own what needed doing—dividing up my increasingly limited time, identifying need I was particularly well suited to address, finding the strategies that seemed most successful, and seeking where possible to bring together my commitments and my career. And then doing the things that might or might not make a difference but seemed critical nonetheless.

Defining "my own" and "my city" were the problems that, like need itself, were not going away. They would never cease from the land. But I could open my hand—my Jewish hand, my American hand, my human hand—to give and to receive without knowing all the answers.

MICHIGAN STATE UNIVERSITY, EAST LANSING, FALL 2011

For eight weeks from late August into October 2011, I do precisely the work I love to do, with twenty students who flower in the sun of new learning and the attention of a teacher who likes teaching.[2]

In spite of my hesitation to set aside my regular course on literacy and historical catastrophe, I have gone forward with a new course. Although I have called it "Truth Telling in American Culture," I know it might just as well be titled, "How to Learn in University." Like all my seminars for freshmen, it is the place where I start to guide students toward adult thinking—the sort of thinking that once started, does not yet know where it will end. The sort of thinking inspired by reading words someone else wrote: someone else who cannot be assimilated into our own identities but who has reached out from some other time or place to say something that has not been lost. We are listening.

On campus, in the classroom, clothes run green and white, a million variations of Michigan State University (MSU) gear. At the beginning of the semester, it's shorts and tank tops, baseball caps and flip flops. Then, as the days get shorter and cooler, it's sweatpants, sweatshirts, scarves, and knit hats. Away from home, away from church, these new students navigate between the classroom and the dorm room, their parents calling, their Facebook alerts are beeping. They are trying to remember to call their teachers "Dr." or "Professor," rather than "Mrs." They are trying to figure out what to do in the hours that still surprise them between classes. Theirs is a new and absorbing life, of which my course is but one part.

◆ ◆ ◆

I woke early those bright fall mornings of 2011. With my husband, Ori, I would gently prod our children awake, though most mornings at least one of them had found their way to our bed in the night. Tzipora was eighteen months. Shai was four and in preschool at the local Jewish Community Center. Priya was in second grade at the Hebrew Day School. Sleep in their eyes, hair mussed by nighttime shifting, we lifted their arms to help them out of pajamas, tied their shoelaces, made lunches, kissed them, tickled them when possible into good moods. We sent Priya and Shai off to school with confidence that they would play and learn, and left Tzipora to our beloved babysitter, Lori, sure that she would eat, sleep, and explore in safety and pleasure.

In the first week of the term—also the Jewish month of Elul, which immediately precedes Rosh Hashanah, the Jewish New Year—I learned the names of twenty new students. College teaching has its own rhythms, one of which is the fourteen-week semester. For fourteen weeks, we would meet twice a week, two hours each time. I would come to recognize their e-mail addresses at a glance and listen to them joke with each other during our short breaks or before class began. When I held office hours, these would be the faces I would see most often. In the classroom, I would detect tiredness, happiness, anxiety, curiosity, boredom. We would come to know each other under these highly particular conditions and I would refer to them as "my students," in that curious mix of the possessive and the anonymous—a phrase that partakes of love and acceptance of responsibility, but also exasperation and no-way-out, the way one says, "my family."

Then the semester would end, and in some cases relationships would have been formed that would last much longer. In other cases, I would never see these people again. I would rarely know what the course amounted to over the passage of time—what remained, what evaporated. I would not know what they remembered of me or of the material. I would be sure that my memories differed from theirs.

I would be one of a limited number of teachers with whom these students had studied, while they would join the hundreds I had taught. Often I would be asked to write recommendation letters because I knew them well given the small class size, and occasionally, I would receive a letter or an e-mail years later, with no purpose but to thank me—to remember out loud, to remind me.

But at the outset of the semester, when I begin to teach, I am not reminiscing. On the contrary, I am intimidated by how much hard work lies ahead of me. I think back to the end of the previous semester and wish I could just reencounter those faces—that last bunch of "my students"—because of how much work we have already done together. But no, here is the new group, and my work lies ahead: the work of coming to know each other and the work of teaching them to read and write.

◆　◆　◆

I had been hired at MSU seven years earlier, in 2004, the week after Priya was born. I joined a small group of faculty in the humanities division of MSU's residential James Madison College (JMC). The focus of the college was public affairs. In practice, this meant that very few of my students were likely to pursue futures in literature or the humanities. My specialized training in Victorian literature would rarely be in demand. But the college prided itself on a demanding and engaging writing program with small seminars taught mainly by tenure-stream faculty. In a market where any academic job at all was something for which to be grateful, I was glad to join a humanities program at a major research university. I was fortunate, too, to have a great deal of freedom in the classroom, freedom that friends of mine teaching in more traditional English departments sometimes envied. I could formulate courses around most of my new ideas and interests so long as I could find a way to make them relevant to a public affairs curriculum.

The truth-telling course was an experiment that came out of the simple observation that many popular American narratives turned on the exposure of a truth. I thought of reality television, plot- or character-driven TV series and movies, novels, investigative newspaper reporting, election politics. Granted, the United States was not alone among cultures in telling these stories. But in the U.S., it seemed to me, you could see that intoxicating combination of the pull of democracy to unearth entrenched interests, the push of individualism to oppose the system, the belief in the ordinary man or woman who can make a difference no matter their social origins, the appeal to a new nation of earnest naïveté and sheer grit, and the belief that we are a place where the good triumphs again and again, refining and perfecting the union. Of course, we are drawn to the drama of the truth.

Teaching at JMC had made me far more conscious about civic education. I was teaching young Americans, in the United States. They would vote for the first time as college students, they would begin a path toward a career as they studied, and their politics would be shaped by what they learned in class and outside of it. Many of them would eventually seek work as policy analysts, lawyers, governmental and nongovernmental organization (NGO) workers, as well as politicians, diplomats, and career military personnel. Although my primary research interests remained focused on Victorian Britain, it made sense to help students study America in a way they might not otherwise: through its contemporary literature.

At summer's end, I had sat with a pencil, notebook, and a stack of books, and sketched out weeks of subunits and selected readings. I divided the semester into truth telling and the military; then truth telling and family; truth telling and education; truth telling and gender; truth telling and the idea of fiction.

I had not come to this material by chance. Over the years I had taught at JMC, I had learned the differences between my new clientele and the English majors I had taught in other universities. *Truth* was remarkably literal for many of my students. While English majors rarely needed to be sold on the merits of fiction, I learned that public affairs students could be dismissive of it, thinking, as Plato had, that fiction was sometimes another word for *lies*. Like Plato, some seemed to believe that fiction was seductive music leading away from truth and noble action or, at best, a harmless distraction from the purposes of the real world, from the truth residing in nonfictional accounts of great men and deeds. In my early years teaching at

JMC, I spent a good deal of time trying to help students consider what truths fiction might be uniquely capable of offering.

But as time passed, I realized that nonfiction was in serious need of attention, too, particularly since students rarely applied anything they learned about fiction to the reading of nonfiction. The postmodern questioning of the boundaries between fiction and nonfiction was not at all part of my first-year students' repertoire. If a book was in the nonfiction category, then it was reliable, could be taken at face value, and begged no "interpretation"; what was there to interpret about facts? Since most had studied history in high school solely from textbooks that rarely featured authors' names with any prominence, they believed that historians presented generally neutral chronicles of past events. The idea of a historical *argument* that contested other carefully considered versions of events was unfamiliar to most of them.

Yet if my first-year students were naive, they were also cynical. At the same time that official history maintained neutrality, all views, they believed, were biased and there was no fact that wasn't a function of political spin. Statistics were cooked, images were photoshopped, narratives were conveniently spliced to serve the teller's interests. These eighteen-year-olds had grown up in an era of intense political polarization. They were children of the twenty-four-hour news cycle; of avowedly partisan news outlets; of the Internet's endless possibilities of representation and the new viability of blog posts written by anyone on any subject, with no fact checking, no review, no standard. They got their news from Jon Stewart and Stephen Colbert, occasionally from their Facebook feed. And they had gotten their history from authorless textbooks and omniscient narrators. This made for some confusion.

I came to see many of these young college students as both unsophisticated and hardened on matters that seemed to me critical to their capacity to become informed citizens and thinking adults. Could it really be that there were *no* facts capable of resisting our desires for them? Could it really be that History spoke in a monotone? As a professor of humanities, teaching students of public affairs, I saw a meeting point for my literary expertise and their liberal, civic education, the education so often defined on university websites as "critical thinking."

It thus became my practice to include autobiographical narrative in all my first-year courses. Here, I would try to separate the inglorious work of indoctrinating a credulous public from the creative, indeed inevitable, work of making meaningful narrative from factual events—to take story elements and employ them in recognizable forms, transforming chronicle to story, as the historiographer Hayden White had described it when he pointed to the shared dimensions of literary and historical writing.[3]

I wanted to show students just how much art went into shaping even seemingly straightforward accounts of historical events, into relating things that had "really happened." Just as a novelist shaped a story from multiple story elements, fashioning them into an arc with meaning and explanatory force, so too did autobiographers and historians take the facts of the past and set them artfully and in good faith into forms of narrative that shaped how we understand them: whether as tragedy, redemption, or ongoing struggle. No set of facts told its own story.

But at the same time, I wanted them to see that there *were* such things as facts, that there were historical realities that no historian, whether personal or professional, could ignore, without being responsible for a story so incomplete or misleading as to constitute culpable falsehood. Some "splicing" was, simply put, lying.

During that summer of 2011, I perhaps did not realize that this material I was organizing held special urgency for me. I did not yet realize that there were specific truths I wanted students to recognize, truths we might call moral. There were truths that in teaching at Beit Rabban, for example, or in teaching my own children in my own home, undergirded all further thought and action. They were truths that *demanded* thought and action. *Hotmo shel ha kadosh barukh hu emet* (The seal of the Holy One, Blessed Be He, is truth), the ancient rabbis taught (Tr. Shabbat 55A). I did not recognize that the civic education that seemed critical to me in the public university overlapped with some of the deepest convictions of my religious life.

The syllabus I was writing was as interleaved with civic and religious elements as the books on my wooden shelves themselves. The American history I had studied in college, the British nineteenth-century novels I had read one after the next in graduate school, and the contemporary memoirs I had collected while writing my own first book were perhaps the bulk of my collection. But I also had books of philosophy, poetry, political economy, anthropology, art history, histories of science, photography, essays, theories of education, religious thought, biography, letters, short stories, and plays.

My office tended to hold mainly the books from which I taught, plus the significant overflow from our home. Even after years of having an office to call my own, I still kept my most beloved volumes, regardless of genre, at home. Two sets of books resided only in our home. Our house held, first, the veritable library of children's books I had been amassing for years, but most intensively since Priya was born. Hundreds of children's books picked one by one, lovingly, specifically, critically. I knew them by spine, I knew them by heart, I knew them by which child of mine loved them best. They were scattered throughout our house, not a room without them. In beds, on the floor, on tables and chairs and shelves.

And then there was the other library in our home: shelves and shelves of holy books, most of them in Hebrew characters. The Hebrew Bible, the Mishnah, the Talmud, the Midrash, codes of law, codes of ethics, philosophy, modern Jewish thought, prayer books for different days and times of year, the Passover Haggadah, psalms, poetry, dictionaries, lexicons, and concordances. Many of these were books you kissed if by chance they touched the floor, books you buried in the earth when they were so well worn they could no longer serve.

I was going to teach a course on truth and America, through books, and this course, more than any other I had ever taught, would remind me that there were some books I kept at home and others in my office. Was there a logic to the separation? Was it sustainable? Did I want to sustain it any longer?

Where did my books take me? Who was I when I read them? Who was I when I taught them?

BARNARD COLLEGE, NEW YORK, 1989–1993

Unpacking the tens of book cartons, the hundreds of books, that we shipped from Ann Arbor to Jerusalem, I find my high school yearbook, almost three decades later. There is my photo ("Ima," with surprise, "you were pretty!"); signatures ("You had a lot of friends! Were you malkat ha-kita [the queen of the class]?"); a past that has been almost buried by all the significant pasts in between. Yet if that past seems momentarily all but someone else's, here is the quotation I chose, by Eudora Welty, bringing me back to myself: "A sheltered life can be a daring life. For all serious daring starts from within."

It had been a sheltered life and I had known it when I left home for the first time. My acceptance to Barnard College arrived in the spring of 1988, on fine, grainy letterhead, a sort I had never received before. Along with the acceptance came a surprise: I had been invited to join a program called the Centennial Scholars, designed to offer a small group of talented students the opportunity to craft an independent project with a mentor over the course of two years. We would also become a community, joining together to study in seminars, as each of us worked on her project. Would I please call the Office of Admissions (collect!) for help booking a free trip to New York to visit the college and meet the other incoming and current scholars.

Barnard in the 1990s offered me a first-class education, enhanced considerably by the camaraderie and intellectual energy of the Centennial Scholars program. In my first semester, we met in an interdisciplinary seminar led by two faculty members, one an economist, and the other, a scholar and translator of Hindi literature. Here, I first encountered the strange, large ideas that converted us from high school students into female denizens of the American university world. We considered how science works; what difference it made to be a woman artist; how cities functioned; what the province of social history was. We read a huge biography of Robert Moses; the work of Stephen Jay Gould on measures of intelligence and racial bias; Virginia Woolf's *A Room of One's Own*; John Berger's *Ways of Seeing*; and as we read, we were inducted into the critical discourses of the late twentieth century.

But always, we were in New York. This happened to be the city my parents had grown up in, and the borough, Manhattan, my mother had known best. My mother's parents still lived across town on the Upper East Side in a rent-controlled apartment they had inhabited since my mother was a teenager, giving her for the first time the privacy of her own bedroom. During my college years, my grandmother, Birdie, would take two buses—the M79 across town, then the M104 uptown—to come feed me. She brought me bread from her neighbors' bakery. She brought me sweet dried apricots, because I had once said that I liked them. She brought me chicken soup, and sweet and sour meatballs in reused plastic containers stacked in large supermarket paper bags. She always took a transfer when she traveled because even if she didn't need the second bus, someone else would, and she could hand it to the next person in line.

I took buses, too, and subways, and walked the city streets with my eyes open. From the islands of time and space of seminar rooms with their heavy, oval wooden tables and reddish Oriental rugs, after teas with the college president and visiting scholars and artists, amidst trips to the Matisse exhibit at the Museum of Modern Art and to Phantom of the Opera on Broadway, the streets of the city looked gray and grim.

In 1990, it was impossible not to see that my neighborhood, Morningside Heights and beyond it, the Upper West Side, was simply full of homeless people. Federal funding of low-income housing had been cut dramatically during the 1980s, as had federal monies designated for city budgets more generally. Now people without homes were sitting on the streets, sleeping on the streets, riding the trains all day and night, camping out in the subway stations and beside bus stops, in the islands on the center of the North-South highway of Broadway. Parks were full of them and you could not walk in or out of any supermarket or small shop without a cup and a hand greeting you, without the request, and sometimes the demand, for help, for money, for food. Thin men wrapped in blankets lay propped against New York City's brick buildings, sleeping in the dim light at 6:30 A.M., when I crossed Broadway to go to daily prayer at Columbia.

Drugs, AIDS, mental illness—I went to college in the midst of a dark reality of suffering, with the margins of experience not at all marginal to the bourgeois frame of vision. In the two churches I visited to feed people and then to throw out their garbage after meals, I noticed the murky, not especially well-crafted images of Jesus suffering on the cross, the barefoot, anonymous poor gathering around him. Those blurry, flat pictures—you could put them on the ground and walk across them without feeling too bad— they were the New York City of the late 1980s and early 1990s.

The professors of the Centennial Scholar seminar gave us a great deal of freedom. And so when they assigned us the task of composing a survey and analyzing our findings, I found myself wondering what it meant to my fellow college students and myself to pass tens of homeless people every single day on our very short paths to class and to the dorm, to the cafeteria and the library and, for some of us, to communal prayer. The gates of Columbia University and Barnard College were open ones, and although beggars did not wander campus (no doubt they were not allowed), they stood right beside the iron gates, by the steps down to the subway, hovering over the gratings where steam rose from below.

My survey asked such questions as: "What is your attitude toward homeless people? What do you perceive the public attitude to be?"

"Do you give homeless people money? Sometimes? Always? Never?"

"Have you ever given a homeless person something that is not money?"

"Have you ever had contact with a homeless person off the streets?"

"Has your attitude toward the homeless shifted since you arrived in New York? At what point did it shift?"

"Have you ever imagined what it would be like to be homeless? Can you imagine a chain of events that would leave you penniless and homeless?"

At the heart of my project was a single question: Does seeing the homeless every day make most of us more or less sensitive to their plight? In the presence of need, do we harden, becoming cynical or choosing not to see, or do we find a way to address need, even if only by talking to people who have no home? What difference does it make to live with good fortune in the midst of poverty?[4]

Today, I do not remember what my findings were. I also barely remember how the questioning went or whom I got to fill out my survey, though I did find my master in the boxes that crossed the Atlantic and the Mediterranean from Michigan to Israel.

What do I remember? My worry that we would stop seeing these people, that they would become invisible to us, or annoying. That we would feel fine walking past them with our own arms full of groceries, our own heated apartments or dormitory rooms waiting for us.

Often, when my grandmother brought me more food than I could possibly eat, I transferred it directly into the hands of the poor who stood so close to my doorway.

BEIT RABBAN, NEW YORK CITY, 1992–1994

I began my teaching career not as a graduate student or an assistant professor, but as a twenty-two-year-old in the last semester of my BA, at a tiny, innovative Jewish school in New York City. My job at Beit Rabban found me and I found it in the kind of mutual recognition that seemed then and seems now providential.

In my sophomore year of college, I had taken a part-time job teaching afternoon school at SAJ (the Reconstructionist Society for the Advancement of Judaism) on West 86th Street and Central Park West. In the fall of 1991, I entered my classroom after a summer away to see immediately that I was now sharing the space with a new tenant. And this tenant did not travel light. The two connected rooms had been transformed, defined, claimed.

For teachers, sharing space is rarely a recipe for success, but as I looked around the room, all I could think was that I wanted in. Something had begun here that was rare and invaluable. Even in the absence of children—perhaps especially in the absence of children—the classroom announced itself as a place built with great care, imagination, and aspiration. What was this school? *Who* was this school?

In the quiet, I walked around the rooms, learning them. First, I took in the absences: there were no store-bought materials on the walls, no cut-outs of fall holiday emblems or images of happy school children returning to their studies. Everything on the walls was made by children, imperfectly, messily, at times even unintelligibly.

There were no bulletin boards boasting "projects" in which each piece of student work had met the clear demands of a teacher. Each bulletin board had a central idea, but it was often articulated in a question, from "How many ways can you connect two dots?" to "What is bread made of?"

Answers were drawn and scribbled, and written in effortful letters: "DO," I took to be "dough." Later, I would come to understand how and why GGG stood for "eggs" and "DR" for "water" (how many of us pronounce the *t* in water, after all?).

And there were books in this classroom, everywhere—books about bread around the world, cookbooks, a book about baking challah for the Sabbath, and a book about the way wheat grew, a book about supermarkets and the transport of goods. Later, I would learn that these books were resources for the children's interdisciplinary unit on plants and food.

On another table were a slew of alphabet books. Then there was what appeared to be a book corner with cushions on the floor. There were shelves that exhibited about fifteen picture books with extraordinary illustrations, about half of them by the same illustrator. There were three long shelves, packed with books whose spines showed many of them to have been used by multiple generations of students. As I began to examine the shelves, all of which a young child could reach, I gathered that another school's library had perhaps been sold or given to this classroom, then mixed with more recent acquisitions. The books were classified into fiction and nonfiction. Within fiction, they were alphabetized by the first letter of the author's last name, which made it easy for children to return books to their place. Within nonfiction, they were sorted by subjects and the shelves were simply, descriptively labeled: "world history," "animals," "biography," and so on.

And there were also labels, in Hebrew and in English. In fact, everywhere I turned in this classroom, I saw labels. They were probably the most noticeable thing of all. "Chair." "Table." "Light." "Door." The words stood out, printed in beautiful bright colors, each letter so clearly drawn it was like a small work of art. Surrounded by simple nouns, suddenly, I felt like a child myself, beginning to read, seeking the one-to-one correspondence between word and world. Each letter was a promise that came together with others to make a word. Sentences lay ahead. Then stories.

Clearly, kids had made some of the labels. Next to them the labels the teacher had made were posted, with standard spelling and letters all the same size.

I could tell from the way this classroom anticipated children—from the way it hosted them, and respected them, and did not condescend to them—that it held the beginning of a life of learning.

Later that day, I had already secured the phone number of the school director. (And this was 1991, before widespread e-mail and Google.) Dr. Devora Steinmetz was a young scholar with a PhD in comparative literature who had recently written a book on biblical literature and had established Beit Rabban in part for her own growing family. She was married to an outstanding educator in his own right, Rabbi David Silber, who had founded the Drisha Institute for Jewish Education in 1979 to fill the gap for women seeking access to and expertise in classical Jewish texts.

Within two days, I had come to observe the school in action. It turned out that I had seen all of it in the two adjoining classrooms I had surveyed. In its first year, the school was a joint kindergarten and first grade. Seven students, from nearly five to six years old, two teachers, and Devora. School hours were 8:30 A.M.–3:30 P.M. Recess was held in Central Park; lunch was eaten at small tables in the classroom. Parents—mothers and fathers—dropped off the children in the morning and a combination of babysitters and parents picked them up at the end of the day. There was no administrative staff yet, no infrastructure. From an institutional perspective, it was the bare bones of a school, but it was also the most thoughtfully designed space for learning I had ever seen.

I came home and prepared to graduate a semester early. The following fall, I began teaching in this classroom.

I can fairly say that I learned to teach at this school over the next two years, working first part-time as I finished college and then full-time after I had graduated. My mother was a teacher, my paternal grandparents had both been teachers, and I had wanted to be a teacher as long as I could remember; still, this job was a greater delight than I could ever have imagined. My coteacher was a fully bilingual young woman who had grown up in Israel and America, and was a natural in the classroom. Her confidence from the previous year spent teaching in the school spilled over to me as we learned to share our responsibilities and coordinate our efforts.

Taly and I taught nearly everything together, from two daily sessions in Hebrew language immersion to prayer to math to community service to a reading-writing workshop to the interdisciplinary units that provided rich opportunities for investigations in social studies, literature, and science. We were both present for snack, which always ran in Hebrew, and recess at the park, which was as much a time for learning as any other time of day. We both circulated in the room during the children's time to choose their own activities, from imaginative play to building, to writing in Hebrew and English, to game playing. Devora was in and out of the classroom constantly, modeling for us conversations with kids as much as more structured learning, and helping us plan our activities so that they were as meaningful as possible. I spent a great deal of my free time reading books she gave me on interdisciplinary education, foreign language immersion, and most formatively, the reading-writing workshop approach.

In the weeks before I began to teach, Devora and I had spent five days in a summer institute at Teachers' College, at the Reading and Writing Project. There, I had gotten my first exposure to the reading-writing workshop, an approach I made my own over the course of my two years teaching full-time at Beit Rabban.[5] As an aspiring writer myself, it was not hard to persuade me that children, too, benefit from experiencing writing as a process; that conferring with a mentor is critical to developing and deepening one's work; that we learn more about writing from inquiring into what we like to read than we learn from abstract instruction; that writing is a rich everyday activity as well as an art. Although I could not have known it then, testing these ideas against daily practice with five- and six-year-olds taught me much of what I needed to know to teach writing at any level.

Ask most teachers and they will tell you that the first year of full-time teaching is unforgettable. In my case, it was unforgettable in the best possible ways. I worked incredibly hard in a setup that was ideal for me and, I believe, for the small group of children we were educating. Twenty-five years later, I recall each of the children by name and remember about many of them things as small and intimate as those a parent remembers about her own precious children. Masha, a recent Russian immigrant, was mischievous, with uneven pigtails and an irrepressible smile; she began the year hiding under the table, understanding no English. Beruria dotted all her *i*'s with Jewish stars or hearts, and for a while, insisted on writing her five names on all her drawings; when we found drawings without names on them, we would go to her for scrutiny and unerring identification. Eli, with his round tummy and blunt looks, loved the poem "Stopping By Woods on a Snowy Evening," and rocked back and forth in my lap as we recited it, while Zach, with his bright red hair and the first pair of glasses in the class (turquoise), wrote a series of very short stories starring a version of himself, "Zach the Detective." The illustrations all featured arrows to signify action.

There are no doubt hundreds, maybe thousands, of good schools in the world, and hundreds, maybe thousands, of innovative and deeply thoughtful school directors, but this was the school I wound up in and this was the one that left its mark on me during the years I learned to teach and began to think about how people learn, and what is worth learning. In my mind, this school in its initial, highly idealistic and intensely concentrated years, remains the model against which I measure other schools.[6]

At Beit Rabban, I learned a critical piece of knowledge for any teacher who thinks she is teaching not only subject matter but human beings. I learned that it helps to know what sort of person you want to help shape and what sort of society you would like to help build.[7] When you have some idea of those guiding ends, you can work backward and begin to consider how to relate to your students. You can start to figure out what and how you would like to teach and what you hope your students will learn. You can plan for the inevitable gap between what you offer and what is likely to be received.

Every classroom posits an outcome, even if it is totally implicit and unconscious. But teaching well has come to mean to me: making it conscious.

READING-WRITING WORKSHOP, BEIT RABBAN

Early in the morning, I sit in a bright room at a small table, absent of children for now. Before me are the tools of the trade: my own notebook and a box of thick wide Crayola markers in primary colors. I write out short poems on the lightly lined, rough, full-size newsprint, the marker bleeding through in reverse formation on the other side of the page.

During the years I taught K-1, I wrote down poems by Carl Sandburg, Robert Frost, William Carlos Williams, Langston Hughes, and Christina Rossetti, as well as the beginnings of the morning prayers Jews around the world recite in Hebrew, blessings that often read like poetry, shaped by parallel structure. I would hang them in our classroom one at a time, exhibiting each new blessing in written form as we learned it. Devora had told me not to hang written things merely as decoration, especially things the children would not yet be able to read themselves, because that bred the habit of ignoring the written word, and in general, of ignoring the environment. Seeing but not seeing was the last thing we wanted. Instead, she suggested that I hang written things I planned to use for specific purposes and that those things should stay on the wall once we had read them together so the kids could return to them as known objects. *Use* the walls, I understood her as saying. Make language speak with urgency and interest.

Sometimes, before the children came in at 8:30 A.M., during the last few minutes of privacy and quiet, I would hang a new poem near the door or on the board, waiting to see who would notice it and try to decode its simple, often monosyllabic words. "Fog comes in on little cat feet...." I would write the name of the author at the bottom in a different color, and children came to remember the names of the poets and the poems associated with them.

Reading-writing workshop, the last hour of the day, started daily in a circle on the floor, with material for reading aloud: this was reading as a starting point for our writing. Sometimes reading aloud and discussing would occupy us for five minutes, and sometimes for almost half the workshop time. In spite of workshop time beginning near the school day's end, children seemed to find it a kind of daily homecoming, a time that was often very energetic, but also peaceful. The pleasures of being read to, coupled with the pleasures of self-expression, within a community of other readers and writers. And there was always the promise that one could continue tomorrow. Nothing was ending with the day's end.[8]

I loved teaching poetry and picture books best, but workshop was hardly limited to those forms. We read models of whatever it was that we became interested in writing and we wrote adaptations of much of what we read: picture books, fairy tales, jokes, sayings, nonfiction books, biographies, alphabet books.

We wrote recipes and lists of all kinds: Lists of all the words in the classroom that began with the letter B. Lists of every vegetable we could think of. Lists of birthdays in the classroom. Lists of middle names. Lists of books we had read aloud.

Then there were letters: Letters to friends in the class, delivered straight from hand to hand. Letters to family members near and far. Letters to experts when we had questions.

Questions were themselves a full-fledged genre in our classroom. Often, they were written on index cards for the question board and concerned things we were learning, as well as anything else in the world. Many of our questions emerged from the study of Torah, where the first exposure to short sections of text was directed toward the children formulating their own questions and then categorizing them (are they factual? interpretive? where might we go for answers for these different kinds of questions?) We generated questions in our interdisciplinary units, and when we worked with manipulatives in math, and when we baked in Hebrew. There were no questions that were off limits.

Kids wrote reports and suggestions for teachers. They wrote newspapers, comics, scrolls, labels, instructions, games, scavenger hunt clues, interviews, crossword puzzles, book reviews, and recommendations. It was all writing.

Our students ranged in age from nearly five to just seven. Some children wrote in all capital letters. Some wrote the same few capital letters over and over, often the dominant sound in whatever word they had in mind, while others, late in the year, wrote in near-paragraphs, with lowercase and uppercase letters, not to mention periods, exclamation points, quotation and question marks. Some of the children earliest in their development dictated to friends or a teacher. Some loved to draw or decorate single letters from their names. But everyone wrote.

There were children who wanted their own writing to be closer to what we called "book spelling," and we encouraged them to work with dictionaries or to build their own lists of words they wanted to know. Other children liked the funniness of homonyms or palindromes and they began to learn to spell in this way. Still others just wanted to write without being interrupted, without any regard yet for conventional spelling. At times, kids wanted to write in Hebrew, which they were just learning, too. The classroom featured Hebrew print as visibly as English.

Books in Hebrew and English lay open beside children who were writing and copying words and phrases—as legitimate and meaningful a way to write as fresh composition. If Emily, intent on book spelling, asked, "How do you spell 'once-upon-a-time'?" all I needed to say back was, "Find a book that begins that way." Reading led to writing, which led to reading, which led to writing.

Kids wrote at tables, on the floor, in the book corner, in the block corner, or in the hallway if they needed more quiet or more space. They wrote standing up and sitting down, and occasionally lying on their stomachs. Sometimes they wrote together, other times, alone. I remember certain weeks when crazes would spread through the classroom and everyone would write "princess books," or ghost stories, recipes, or news articles, and I would get out multiple models of each of these kinds of writing and we would look at them closely, together: What did they have in common? What was the nature of this form?

For kids having a hard time coming up with ideas or getting started, there was what became for me the tried and true, "I write a line, you write a line." Let's share the page. Let's talk through writing.

Ari would write a single thought, then I would write a single thought back. I would pose a related question, and move over to help another child while he considered an answer. Then he wrote it down, and often followed up with another question, this time posed to me. Other kids, seeing our "conversation," began following me around with clipboards, wanting to talk this way as well. Later, when I began to teach university, it would take time for me to realize that many students did not presume that a chief purpose of writing was to communicate, that it beckoned for an audience, for response.

The classroom was stocked with many writing materials, which were available during workshop but at all other points during the day as well.

Notebooks, sheets of lined paper, unlined paper, newsprint paper with lines and space for illustrations above, small stapled books, bookmark-size paper, clipboards. We offered many choices, carefully considered, because we knew there were many different ways to write. Different forms made their own demands.

Although I had been writing most of my life, I had never seen so vividly the way material made a difference until I worked with very young writers. One day, Masha proudly read me the story she had written in English. It was a slowly developing princess tale, which I listened to with great pleasure until, with no warning, it suddenly ended, as if the lights had just gone out in a storm.

"Oh my goodness," I said, genuinely surprised, "I wasn't expecting your story to end just then."

Masha looked at me, this small, bright child, and explained simply, "It had to end because there's no more room on the page. Look how small I wrote at the bottom."

Tiny letters spelled out, "THE END," at the very bottom of her single page.

Together, we went to the shelves with supplies and added a second page. I offered her the hole puncher and pins to attach the pages, because then the story could go on as long as she might ever want it to. I showed her how to number a second page. This was the kind of teaching I loved, teaching that took nothing for granted, that looked and listened to see how a child—this child—thought, then tried to give her what she needed to do more, to see her way forward.

Together, we erased "THE END," and Masha resumed her story.

In workshop, I learned when it was time to help and when it was time to make myself scarce. I learned to let kids solve their own problems or simply develop their own plans and projects, or to work together, helping each other, sometimes simply by example. I watched for the right moments to step forward to provide new information to individual kids or groups, information that might help make their writing more easily understood by readers. We drew their attention to the spaces (or lines or dots) between words that made sentences legible and to forms of punctuation visible in the books they read (quotation marks: characters speak!).

When a few children had worked hard enough over a few days on a single piece of writing, I brought in samples of my own multiple drafts, both printed and handwritten pages, marked up and altered. I showed them words I had underlined or crossed out, question marks in the margins, arrows and asterisks shifting the position of a sentence or paragraph. As they held my pages in their hands, I explained, "This is how editing works."

One day, we brought in a local artist to show the kids her boards for a counting book she had illustrated. She showed them the boards, the bright images of fruits, one through ten, oranges and watermelons, there on the floor beside the kids. Our job was to show them the steps from here to there.

Writing had its frustrations. When one child couldn't manage all her papers, we weighed the relative benefits of paper clips and staples; we found folders, binders, and ribbons. When another child came back to school distressed that his parents could not read his story, he read it back to us, and we put conventional spelling underneath his own print. We encouraged him to be the reader, and his parents the listeners, instead of the other way around. We explained our rationale to his parents and he practiced reading it aloud to other kids before taking it home again. A child who could not yet read, memorized a poem and recited it for all of us.

Our world of language was large and forgiving. It had room for all of the students, all of us. Perhaps most important, we were in no rush. I did not worry that the children would not learn to read or write or spell. As I wrote out those poems in the mornings, hearing them in my head in the quiet classroom, I knew I could rely on words and their music, on images in the mind, on native intelligence and curiosity.

I also did not worry about filling the time. There was so much to work with.

MICHIGAN STATE UNIVERSITY, FALL 2011

I opened "Truth Telling" with Anthony Swofford's *Jarhead: A Marine's Chronicle of the Gulf War and Other Battles*, a book I had read only once, a rarity for me when I taught. I had owned it for many years, a remaindered copy bought off a table on New York's West Side, from a time in my life when I bought books more regularly than I bought milk. I had read it in early August 2011 before the school year began and decided that it earned its violence and nearly nonstop profanity. It seemed well worth teaching. At the very least, it was a good book to start with since all the swear words would alert the freshmen to the fact that they were not in high school any-more, that their teacher could handle *motherfucker*, and even say it out loud in the classroom, if necessary.

Jarhead took my class by storm. They loved it. First, it did not bore them. They seemed truly appreciative of assigned reading that held their interest. But mostly, they were moved by the sense that someone was talking straight with them, giving them a story that was not censored or made official or "educational" in the traditional sense. These were students, after all, who had been visited by recruitment officers at college fairs and who were con-nected to the armed forces by more than the thin tether that I was. We played the web advertisement for the U.S. Marines on the classroom screen. We considered its promises and its images in light of Swofford's account, not to denigrate the U.S. Armed Forces or to accuse them of lying, but to consider the author's education and evolution in the realities of warfare and violence.

Some students were genuinely shocked by what this former marine recounted. A few were surprised by how bitter he seemed and how little stock he put in categories such as "heroism," "sacrifice," and "patriotism." In a classroom in which every student spoke aloud (we went around the entire circle of eighteen at least once a week), no one expressed or appeared to repress anger at the book, even the cousin of a soldier who had just returned from Iraq, who nodded as I read passages aloud, and reported that he was grateful his cousin had "come back okay."

As for me, I was surprised that the students found the book so eye-opening. Was it really news for a battle-seasoned marine to doubt the neces-sity of his service or the national mission on which he had embarked? To regret his enlistment? To recognize the sickness that war and violence demand and produce?

Perhaps at eighteen, I thought, regret itself is novel. This was not merely a passing thought. I was teaching *Jarhead* as an instance of truth telling not only for its content but for its form, memoir. *Jarhead* begins with the narra-tor opening up his military rucksack and feeling the grains of sand still lodged in its canvas, watching shreds of a tattered map of Iraq flutter to the ground. Through the image of this well-traveled rucksack, the memoir cap-tured both the naive self who had set out for war in Iraq and the man who had come back and, years later, written his memoir. The simple letter *I* was supposed to stand for both selves.

Slowly and painstakingly, the students and I identified the complicated weave of memoir: the distinction between the "I" who was narrating and the "I" who was being narrated, the "I" of the present, seeking to bring back to life the "I" of the past vividly, honestly, yet without ever losing his hold on the present. The narrative reflected to us the technical and existential challenge of a present-tense self, mining the past for an earlier self who had known less, understood much less, than did the sober self, now sitting down to write.[9]

I had read probably close to one hundred memoirs and written one of my own; my students had read few, some of them had read only this one. Together, we encountered the fundamental drama of memoir: there was a time I knew less and now I know more, and I would like to dramatize how I came to know more and share the knowledge acquired, so that the reader too may benefit from it, minus the labor, and often the pain, of living my particular circumstances. This, I have come to think, is why we read memoir: we are looking for that knowledge gained, that difference between the time narrated and the instance of narration.

"Memoir is so complicated," said one student to me. "I would never have guessed."

This put a smile on my face because I had been working on the "complicated" for nearly twenty years and he had just met it for the first time. But together, over two weeks, we watched a narrator inquire into his personal history with curiosity, anxiety, doubt, and some satisfaction. We witnessed the sort of intrepid introspection that does not presume to know what it will find before it sets out.

The students got it—I could hear it and see it around the room—and I felt the particular happiness of successful teaching. With the simple terms "narrating 'I'" and "narrated 'I,'" words written in white chalk on the simplest teaching technology, the blackboard, my students had been initiated into a more sophisticated way to read.[10] They had also achieved the new and important recognition that reading has its higher methods, too.

I believed then as I believe now that almost all the students got it because it was not just a technical lesson in the study of narrative; it was a truth about living: While we are in some way the same people in the present as we were in the past—typically, we retain the same name and often the same basic features of appearance—we are not identical to our past selves. I thought of the way that under normal conditions, we experience our bodies as familiar over time, and yet we know that the cells that make up our bodies are regularly replaced. This is not a simple idea, but perhaps strangely, it is an intuitive one, and a profound one, that is worth the time it takes to see its logic.

By the time I was done teaching *Jarhead*, I felt exhausted, out of breath as if I had scaled a mountain. I had come into the classroom with what I saw as an extremely difficult mission: to convey the pulsing drama of engaging with one's life in language. This was not the drama of cops-and-robbers or an adventure movie or a romance. It was a drama made of spiritual and intellectual stuff, one that was sometimes silent and always private, even if it happened in public. It reminded me of what George Eliot had written about the dawning of an intellectual passion:

> most of us who turn to any subject with love remember some morning or evening hour when we got on a high stool to reach down an untried volume, or sat with parted lips listening to a new talker, or for very lack of books began to listen to the voices within, as the first traceable beginning of our love.[11]

I had been asking students to join me in caring for that kind of low-profile but momentous intellectual discovery. Given the world in 2011, it took a good deal of energy to walk into a room of twenty teenagers, fresh out of not particularly fantastic high schools, and sell them on intellectual passion. I had given it all I had. And they had taken, and given much back.

BEIT RABBAN, WINTER 1992–1993

In year two of the school, the kindergarten through second-grade students are studying "Buildings and Homes." I am surprised by how rich this topic is, though I am learning that real interdisciplinarity makes a great many topics richer than I could have imagined.[12] Devora has been clear that interdisciplinarity isn't window dressing but instead will require us to make connections that draw on the methods and central concerns of different disciplines. Then we can consider the relations among the perspectives of disciplines, too. In the world as we know it, our experience isn't divided up into math, then literature, then social studies, in recognizable, separate packages. We want learning inside the school to be relevant to a life that presents us with diverse and multifaceted problems to solve.

Taly and I sit together, cutting out twenty or so photos of dwellings of all sorts from old copies of *National Geographic* and a few other magazines with beautiful glossy pages. We have images of tents, shacks made of tarps and sticks, igloos, fishing huts, skyscrapers, ranch houses, farmhouses, towers, castles, governmental buildings, the White House, pyramids, a sukkah. We take these images and paste each one individually onto colorful pieces of construction paper. Some we hang on the walls the day before we begin the unit; others we leave on the small circular table located near where kids will enter the room in the morning. Each day, they are greeted with a small selection of books on the rug—books specially chosen as they relate to our subject, or a morning challenge, that is, a task or question to open the day. Today the challenge will be "What do you observe in these pictures?" Alongside this open-ended message, we will leave pencils, crayons, and paper. Kids will congregate and look and write, and look and write more.

I am excited. All these images give me a sense of how much we can learn. As we write the challenge, I realize how much there is to observe, not only the materials with which these structures are built, which is itself a multifaceted question, but also whether there is surrounding vegetation or animal life, and if so, what sort. Are there people? What are they wearing? What is the climate? How might the climate be related to the structure? What is man-made in the picture? What is natural? What is the structure suited for? Is it a place in which people dwell or work? Is it a public or a private space? Can you tell how old the structure is? Is it intended to be permanent or temporary, or something in between? What sort of weather can these structures withstand? What other kinds of structures can we imagine outside the frame of the photo?

Versions of these questions might be other morning challenges, but for now, they help us consider the wealth of possible investigations from which to choose. Some kids might be fascinated by the differences between cities and rural spaces. Other kids might want to know why and how buildings stand up and don't fall down, why some are tall and some are wide. What is an architect? How much time does it take to prepare a dwelling and how many types of worker are involved?

These initial forays make it easy to see that limiting and ordering is an ongoing challenge of interdisciplinary learning when you have a fertile subject, one that genuinely demands and benefits from consideration through the lenses of many disciplines. In the end, we will organize the unit around a few core questions, that is, a "scope and sequence of questions," that will determine the activities we plan.[13] These questions will help us avoid jumping around without purpose, guide us as to when and where to move next.

We brainstorm our topic, "buildings and homes," in relation to a wide range of disciplines. When it comes to math, I know what we will *not* be doing. We won't be counting images of buildings on the page of a worksheet, or learning addition by asking, "If you add one hammer to two hammers, how many do you have?" That sort of connection that can pass for interdisciplinary learning is arbitrary; it is the window dressing approach we avoid.

Instead, we try to work from *inside* each discipline's methods and constitutive concerns. We use the theme to deepen our understanding of the discipline and we believe that the theme would be impoverished if we didn't consider it through the discipline. (Not every theme lends itself equally to every discipline, but part of the work of choosing a theme is making sure that it allows for meaningful exploration in many disciplines.)

In practice, thinking about "buildings and homes" mathematically means we might consider the stability of different shapes. We might map the school's street with respect to its buildings. Students could map their own streets, or even just their home and its rooms. We could study scale, a category intrinsic to the discipline of math. When it comes to geography, we might investigate different climates and their constraints and opportunities, and what social structures result. As for science—it all seems to be science, but we can investigate different materials that are used in building. Cement, clay, mud, wood, brick, glass, and fabric immediately come to mind.

I consider the specialized terms of building and planning. Kids love to learn highly specific words, and fancy words: I have already encountered a few terms that are entirely new to me: I predict that *crenellations*, for example, will be a big hit among the castle and fortress fans. The *blue* in *blueprint* takes us back to the chemistry of early printing. We could study particular architects or invite a local architect to speak with us. We could study some of the amazing buildings of New York City: the Guggenheim, the Empire

State Building. We could ask whether the Statue of Liberty counts as a building.

We will be writing constantly as we work on these ideas, and I imagine that many hours of reading-writing workshop will be devoted to some version of "Building Books." Taly and Devora and I cull the shelves for books about houses and buildings, and Devora invests precious resources in buying new books that will enrich our study.

Beyond finding books full of information, we suddenly recognize just how much this subject shapes the literature we read. Certain genres take place in certain kinds of houses, buildings, eras, and landscapes. What difference would it make if a fairy tale took place in an apartment building rather than a castle? Meanwhile, the entire concept of "neighbors"—our social understanding—is shaped by how we organize our dwellings. Do good fences make good neighbors? Earlier in the year, we studied Frost's poem, "Stopping by Woods on a Snowy Evening," and Eli learned it by heart. The poem begins by noting an absentee landlord ("Whose woods these are I think I know"), and then considers the difference between the owner ensconced in his private house in the village and his dark woods, which feel hospitable to all. Through this new lens, I see now that this poem of snowy solitude in a silent, crystalline world is also a poem about ownership and boundaries, property and privacy. We can return to this poem now and read it fresh.

And like all the subjects we investigate at Beit Rabban, we investigate this one, too, as Jews. The very name of the school, "Beit Rabban," which translates as "our teacher's house," emphasizes how important place is to purpose and to activity.

Always trying to draw links to what we have learned in other contexts (the idea being that we don't "finish" studying a subject), we return to thinking about our study of Sukkot, the autumn harvest holiday in which Jews build temporary structures to represent the shelters in the desert during the Exodus from Egypt. The biblical commandment is to "dwell" (*teishvu*) in the sukkah. What activities constitute dwelling? What does it mean to dwell, but in a temporary shelter? If a sukkah is meant to be impermanent, are we allowed to use nails? Bolts? How do we protect ourselves from the elements in the sukkah? What if it snows or rains? In the climate of the area between Egypt and Israel, where the original sukkot were built, was there a risk of snow?

And what about our permanent homes: How do Jews consecrate their homes? What is the meaning of a *mezuzah* on the doorpost? What do you do if you move out of a house where you have affixed a *mezuzah*? Why is there a commandment to set a fence around one's roof?

Questions arise, too, around the distinction between private and public spaces, and those in between: from courtyards and stairwells to interiors to roofs. We might ask why, given that there is a prohibition to carry items on Shabbat, it is permissible to carry them within the space of one's house. Can we take them outside to the yard if there is a yard? What about down our block?

And then there are the legends: we have cave legends about the ancient rabbis and legends about palaces, waiting rooms, and outdoor ruins. In such legends, place and time seem intimately linked. How, we might ask, can different places describe an ethical or even an existential stance?

And, finally, we will come to the quintessential biblical building, the Tabernacle that comes up during the weekly Torah readings at this time of year. Why is so much ink spilled on the tiniest details of how this structure should be erected and what it should contain? What vision of the world do these directions reflect? What are the relations between the biblical and modern Hebrew word, *shakhen,* neighbor, and the name for the Tabernacle, *mishkan,* and the idea of God's presence as the *shekhina?* What other words come from this root? If all the children of Israel volunteer items and skills to bring to the building of the Tabernacle, is it a collective dwelling? Is it God's dwelling or humanity's? What processes consecrate a space? How do we know when a building is "finished"?

Versions of these questions will no doubt come up during our weekly sessions when we sit together and generate questions for our families to discuss concerning the Torah portion that Jews around the world read simultaneously as the annual calendar unfolds. It is a pleasure for me to know that next year when the children return to those Torah readings, the knowledge they glean from studying buildings and homes may return to them as well. This is learning that mixes readily with life.

The unit will last two months, and when it is done, it will be clear to us all how much more there is that we might still investigate. When you want to teach kids, when you respect and trust their imaginations and intelligence, you wind up learning an immense amount yourself. The world seems fascinating. All things seem connected. Anything seems possible.

MICHIGAN STATE UNIVERSITY, 2011

By late September, the course was well underway. *Jarhead* had proven a compelling text with which to begin our work. With a first text, virtually all my energy went to developing habits of intent listening and intelligent discussion. Our collective findings in discussion would serve as a model for the kind of critical essays I would ask students to write.

Now, when I read sections aloud, as I frequently did, I could see almost all of them following the prose with their eyes, a few underlining or making notes simultaneously. And they were getting more used to the idea of rooting their responses in particular passages from the text.

This was important progress, but even more significant was the work of establishing the norms of our classroom. Just as at Beit Rabban, it had been fundamental for students to learn to listen to each other, to wait until another child was finished speaking before raising their own hands with eagerness; here, too, I insisted on the same policy. I said it clearly on the first day and a few times afterward, when I could see it had not taken hold: if your own hand is up, most likely you are no longer listening well to the person speaking. Please wait until the person has finished speaking. Please do not rush them by waving your own hand as they are trying to think and speak. If you are afraid you will forget your idea, jot down a word or two.

This was not merely a physical policy, though it was amazing to see how difficult it often was for students to bring down their hands, which shot up almost automatically in the very middle of other students' words. (When you are used to a classroom where students do not raise their hands while others are talking, it becomes actually unsettling to see how little store one student sets in another's opportunity to express him- or herself fully.) I would make very small motions to such students to lower their hands, indicating with my eyes that I saw them, that I wouldn't forget, while I kept my focus on the student speaking. Practices like these were as critical to me as any academic learning.

As counterintuitive as these habits were to many of my new students, within a few weeks, I could see that they were starting to listen well not only to me but to each other. They saw that I wrote down in my notebook things that they themselves said when I wanted to remember them. I took notes on *their* ideas; it was not only the other way around.

Slowly, they were beginning to comment on what another student had said using his or her name, as I did, instead of always saying, "like they said," pushing an elbow vaguely in the direction of another student. Enough times interrupting them with a reminder of the other student's name ("you mean James?") led to some inroads. (Still, how far a distance this was from the world of Beit Rabban in which five-year-old Beruria had happily identified other kids' drawings or handwriting in their absence by their personal "style.")

Occasionally, if a student seemed clearly to be addressing only me and waiting only for my reaction to his ideas when he spoke, I would purposely avert my eyes. "Talk to the group," I was saying.

At times, I would say this aloud, too. I made no secret of my aims in discussion, of my sense that we were building a community, exploring an ideal of immersed, active learning. On the contrary, reflecting aloud on these decisions and practices was essential to my purposes.

At the same time that I drew the students' attention to the rhythms and relations of discussion (not constantly, but when it felt helpful), it was also true that moderating this kind of discussion was no longer something I needed to think about when I taught. The habits now ran deep. They shaped me as a teacher, as a person, and as a thinker from the inside out. They were ingrained and embodied my sense of communal study and mutual respect.

Specifically, they embodied my belief that learning did not direct itself toward the aim of pleasing or impressing the teacher, who would inevitably disappear and be exchanged for the next one; who would, in the best case, become a powerful memory rather than a living presence. Learning would happen when one could momentarily forget the teacher and oneself, and become engrossed in the challenges and delights of the subject. It had been my experience that in those moments of forgetting myself, I felt most unself-consciously myself.

A month into this course, which met twice a week for two hours, it had begun to work. Discussion had begun to bear a real rhythm. Students' comments regularly responded to a previous statement made by another student instead of coming out of nowhere, spoken as if in a vacuum of self. Often, students made reference to ideas we had discussed the session before, prompted by my habit of opening most classes by summarizing the previous class discussion, often making reference by name to particular comments individual students had made. (The habit of summarizing was important to me, too, because it modeled how one might take the tangled threads of genuine discussion and, with some work, articulate clear ideas, even a thesis, that had emerged and was worth remembering.)

In this classroom, we were not exactly becoming friends, as children might in elementary school classrooms, but we were nevertheless twenty people coming to know each other in a very particular context. We were building a repertoire of ideas and of shared experience. We had a history of talk. In my mind, we were busy building trust.

Typically in my courses, I confined myself to teaching the writing of critical essays or analytical research papers, believing that those forms were demanding enough in themselves to need at least a full semester's practice. But our work on *Jarhead* had pushed things in a different direction. For the first time, I decided to open up the sort of writing I was teaching and ask students to write from within their new literary knowledge. To learn its challenges from the inside, if possible, and so to appreciate its practice even more.

I told them we were each going to write a personal essay that examined a past instance whose meaning we understood differently today than we had when it happened. In other words, we were going to practice writing an essay in which "I" encompassed both the narrated self and the narrating self, looking back with new knowledge or a changed perspective.

We began in class, sitting quietly. I asked students to jot down for themselves a few instances in their past that now looked different to them. I gave them twenty minutes for this work; I guessed it would be difficult.

These students had gotten into Michigan State not by virtue of curiosity and questioning, but by learning what they had been supposed to learn over twelve years of education. They were mainly obedient students, not defiant. They had learned to write five-paragraph essays that made a claim in the introduction, proved it in three ways, and repeated it in the conclusion. They themselves described being taught to the test (this was the first year of students who had come up from kindergarten through twelfth grade under the teaching practices of No Child Left Behind) and I spent much of their freshman year trying to unteach them.

By that semester in 2011, I knew my student body pretty well. Semester after semester, I looked out at classrooms full of mostly white, nominally Christian midwestern high school graduates, most of them from public schools. From talking to students, I had learned that many parents worked multiple jobs and that many students were themselves working through college and taking summer courses at community colleges to cut costs and time-to-graduation. I looked at my students and saw middle-middle-class kids, and some working-class ones. Fewer were the upper-middle-class and the wealthy I'd come to know when I had taught at other universities. There were very few African American students (7 percent of the university's students were African American, though 14 percent of the state population was black); many fewer Asian American students than I was used to; a handful of Latino students (4 percent in both cases, respectively exceeding and matching state population percentages); and a growing cadre of international students.

Within MSU, James Madison College students tended to be an unusually hardworking bunch, seeking the rigorous education for which the college was known: lots of reading and writing, no easy As, faculty who were devoted to residential undergraduate education. The college was set up in a self-selective fashion: any student who was accepted to MSU could choose to attend JMC as long as there was still a spot. And so we welcomed annually some of the university's top students from Michigan's private and public high schools; at the same time, in a fashion that distinguished JMC from the highly exclusive liberal arts colleges around the country, we also welcomed middle- and even bottom-tier students who had gotten into MSU by the skin of their teeth and were determined to make the very most of their unprecedented and precious opportunity.

The democracy of JMC was directly rooted in the land-grant philosophy of the university. The university had been founded in 1855 as an agricultural college. Since most students came from rural high schools, the curriculum purposely did not include Latin and Greek studies. Students were required to do three hours of daily manual labor to keep down costs for themselves and the institution. A few years later in 1862, the federal Morrill Act was passed, which allocated land for agricultural colleges and the institution became a prototype for sixty-nine land-grant colleges that were then established. The Morrill Act expressed the charge to "teach such branches of learning as are related to agriculture and the mechanic arts, in such manner as the legislatures of the States may respectively prescribe, in order to promote the liberal and practical education of the industrial classes in the several pursuits and professions in life."[14]

The students in the classroom struck me at times as a modernized Rock-wellian postcard of America. Most believed that hard work would be rewarded and that the United States was the best country in the world, with the most opportunity—and they themselves worked hard. They sought opportunities. They were respectful and disciplined; they were impressive, but, with few exceptions, they were not worldly. Very few had passports. Most had lived in Michigan all their lives. When I told students I had studied at Columbia, most assumed I meant Columbia College in Chicago. The Midwest had set the limits to their imaginations.

When I asked these students for personal essays, I knew that I was work-ing against a deeply ingrained ethos. I was seeking risk and curiosity and complexity, essences that I knew were as foreign to many of them as the countries they had never seen. They had all written personal essays to get into college; some of them had written essays to win scholarships as well. I knew how those essays read because I had judged piles of them, struggling to stay awake. They had aimed to present themselves as good citizens, to impress the reader with their capabilities, and to teach or show some kind of moral or lesson learned, in broad strokes.

Here I was asking for something else altogether. I was asking for a portrait that might mean a past failure, at the very least a failure to under-stand themselves or another, or a situation, as fully as hindsight might later allow. True, this too could lead to an essay neatly concluding with "the moral of the story," but we had just read *Jarhead*, and they had seen that there was no sugary moral there. There was something learned, but its price was high and clear. What had been learned was not something easily passed on or easily put into words. I was also asking them to write like good fiction writers and include the sensory details that would bring another world to life for a reader—to include quirks and imperfections, the rough textures of real life. I was asking them to write well.

I told them the truth, adult to adult, that boring was the enemy—that not to be boring took serious effort, especially if they had never before felt the demands of honest, independent reflection. I told them that they would have to write something that began nowhere, in a kind of mist; they should feel they were discovering something *as they wrote*. I guessed they didn't have any idea what I meant when I said that. If they had come to understand that *Jarhead* was about a difference between a past and present self, they had not yet come to understand that the author had figured out the difference *in the writing.* That writing wasn't separable from the knowledge differential, but integral to it. That was part of why I had assigned this writing task: to show them where writing itself fit into the work of self-knowledge and a deepened knowledge of the world in which one lived. I was shooting high and I knew it.

But I believed in these students. I liked them. Our discussions on *Jarhead* had impressed and invigorated me. I had left them excited and satisfied that something good was happening for these college freshmen, something new that justified and defined the transition from high school to the world of the university, that was also their entry into adulthood.

And so I assigned drafts. Nearly automatically, students raised hands to ask how long the papers should be. I said about five to six pages. Many of them looked at me as if I were crazy.

One young woman voiced what many, it turned out, were thinking and said, "Um, Professor Blumberg, I'm pretty sure mine couldn't be longer than, like, a page and a half, max."

"Enlarge the font and margins," I said, and there was silence in the classroom. "I'm kidding," I said.

"I imagine that in many of your high schools you probably found ways to reach an assignment length by padding your work, but here, just write what you need to say and then we can consider how you might expand on your beginnings. Just write what needs to be written."

I was not trying to be mystical. I simply wanted to convey the idea that we were for real here. I knew and they knew that grades would be given, that this was still a classroom with requirements leading to degrees and all that, but this writing assignment was for fellow adults, for writers, for human beings.

Drafts came in and, as I had expected, they were as subtle as bumper stickers. They attested to the love of family, nation, and all humanity; there was not an ounce of the unexpected, not the slightest marker of the distinctive. One student wrote about how his autistic younger sister taught him to appreciate his own good fortune. Another student wrote about how his dad took him fishing and how all he wanted was to grow up to be as good a man as his dad. A third student wrote about how when her dad was out of work, they had not gotten along, but through it all, she knew he loved her and that blood is thicker than water.

There is almost always a moment of disappointment for me when I read first drafts. I generally like my students a great deal in the classroom. They say insightful things and then those things become more insightful as we discuss them. Then, I read their prose and I feel little tendrils of dislike and impatience that I need to let out before I can find within myself the desire to help.

Where in these drafts were my sensitive readers of *Jarhead*? The students who got it, who knew the difference between telling the truth and telling the official story? I, too, believed in the power of family love, of solidarity in hard times, and so on, but I did not believe in these versions.

I didn't comment on the drafts in writing. We came back to class and I talked briefly about the risks of strong writing. The risks of what we might think if we wrote without conclusions at the ready. I said that I was not suggesting that all stories were fundamentally unhappy but that unhappiness and struggle were part of the human condition and to leave them out or to suggest that they could be quickly or easily resolved was not really telling the truth, as I saw it, at least.

Then I read them a section of my own memoir that had come out a few years earlier in which I described real conflict between myself and my mother, whom I loved very much and with whom I had disagreed in ways that tore us apart as I grew into an independent adult. I debated before reading my own work, not wanting to take advantage of a captive audience. But in the end, I decided that if I was asking these students to trust me with real stories, they needed to see first that I had taken such risks myself, and second, that I would trust them with my story.

When I had taught five- and six-year-olds at Beit Rabban, my rule had been that when they wrote, I wrote, too. If they read their work aloud, I needed to be willing to read mine aloud, too. The experience of teaching is so different from that of learning that these few efforts to do the same thing at the same time had seemed important to me. They helped me remember the sense of labor, and sometimes anxious performance, unique to being a student, and I hoped they conveyed to students that I was really with them, involved with them in learning at that very moment.

The room was silent as I read. It occurred to me later that I might have been the first writer, that is, the first published writer, that some of them had ever met, and that I was almost certainly their first teacher who had written a book they could buy on Amazon or at Barnes and Noble. I explained the context of the passage I had selected and then read the two pages slowly. I read it twice so that they could take it in.

The room stayed silent when I was done. I knew it would be impossible to discuss my work out loud so I asked them to write back to me about it. They could write anonymously. I told them I hoped they would consider their own evolving essays as they wrote. For ten minutes, the room remained silent as pencils and pens scratched paper and fingers tapped keys.

"You have to be brave," Kay wrote. "It is not easy to think truthfully and honestly about your own family, but it must be done."

Well, I thought, as I read, it isn't always true that it must be done, but if you feel it must be done, then yes, it must be done. Then other students spoke up:

Andrew: "I think it was a mistake to be so harsh about the mother. She is allowed to think what she wants. Why does the daughter have to criticize her for it?"

Dillon: "You are an awesome writer, I can picture it exactly, I know just what a fight is like and how terrible it is afterward."

Anonymous: "I think I will go back to my essay and it needs a different ending."

Anonymous: "I don't know how to write my own essay better but I know the incident I'm writing about matters. I just realized that I am not sure why it matters."

Maria: "I don't want to be mean to my father in my story but I don't think the way he treated me was fair. I wouldn't want him to read what I wrote and that makes me feel like I shouldn't write it. GUILTY."

Yes, I thought, the ball is rolling.

Here are my *Jarhead* readers, students who can be helped to stop for a moment being preoccupied with seeking admission and scholarships and internships, all highly valuable, even critical things, but not the only things. Here are human beings who are seeking to move into new territory.

For two weeks, we worked on these essays. We talked about revision— real revision—not the addition of periods or commas where they had been missing, not the go-to thesaurus function for fancier word choice, or the crossing out and correction of grammatical mistakes. Revision, instead, in the sense of seeing again, that is, rereading one's own work as a critic to identify the very terrain of the essay: its subject and one's approach to it.[15]

In such a revision, I tried to explain, the units of words, and even sentences, come later. One is after the whole: the idea of the essay, the point of its writing. In this case, revision might mean adding as much as it meant cutting; it would require the writer to consider order—to balance and rebalance as if hanging a fragile mobile that needed strength and tension to fly.

I gave the students a full week for revision, not least to clarify the scale of labor (one or two days would not be enough) and I asked them to hand in their first drafts alongside their revisions, so I could see the two side by side. I told them I would read using both hands.

"Try," I said, "to make real change. The more different your drafts are, the more likely it is that you will receive a high grade."

I hated talking like this but I knew where I was.

"What if it gets worse instead of better?" Kay asked.

Around the room, heads nodded in agreement.

"It's possible," I said, "but I can tell you from my experience that that is a rare thing. How about if we agree that if your essay gets worse, you'll get the chance to switch it back?"

I didn't even engage the question of what worse meant, and how one could tell worse from better. Change was what I was after. Reconsideration.

After I got the second drafts, I took myself to my daughter Priya's room, which had been my study before our other children were born and continued to be the place I was happiest working. The October sunlight was coming in through the two windows, filtered through the purple maple and the pine trees in our neighbors' yard, and Priya's bed was neatly made with its turquoise comforter and the soft pillows she had chosen. I knew she was safe at school.

I organized the papers on her desk—our desk—and straightened the books on the shelf. I made myself a strong cup of coffee and in the quiet morning hours, sitting in the chair by the window, I went through the drafts.

There was movement.

I wrote back to students at some length, making sure to comment particularly on the comparison between drafts, making sure to pose questions, and to do the thing I always try to do: find the one or two elements that offer significant potential for expansion or transformation.

When I was in college, my teacher and mentor, the writer Mary Gordon, had said many times to us that the thing most young writers needed to learn was simply to slow down. Not to rush on or rush past moments that needed slower, more sensitive, and often loving attention.

I have come to feel that this sort of slowness is love. Love for your subject, for the act of writing, for your reader. Slowing down.

In teaching, I came to couple Mary's advice with the phrase of another friend who was sold on the idea of "nuggets." When I read essays, I go searching for the buried good thought that can organize an entire paper. If I can find it, then I can hand it back to the writer, and if they are willing to work hard, they can start writing their paper again, in service of that particular insight. This is enormously difficult for young writers.

And so I read these drafts with the kind of care I bring to my own writing, because it seemed to me that the students were striving, and that they deserved the attention. I work this way on most student essays in writing courses, but these essays called out special care from me because they were about the families and homes the students came from. They were manifestations of the kids themselves.

And they did seem to me like kids—someone else's kids, certainly, but as I read, my sense of the world as a parent and as a caretaking adult was inseparable from my work as a teacher.

I knew my students were adults and that my role was not in loco parentis. I was aware and appreciative of my professional boundaries. I would never have sought to counsel them on the actual dilemmas or dramas reflected in their work.

Instead, I treated their essays as essays. I took pains to refer to the "I" of the work as much as possible as "the narrator," in spite of it being also them—Maria, Dillon, Andrew—the students at my desk. But for all the precautions and the necessary distances, I felt myself teaching them as people and I hoped I was up to the task.

The next week, I met with each student individually for ten to twelve minutes. I had discovered over years of teaching that even if I wrote what felt to me like highly descriptive comments, much was lost on a student if he or she did not hear what I thought out loud, in dialogue. I was committed to these essays and these writers, and I did not want the hours I had already put in to go to waste.

We met in my office, with my walls covered floor to ceiling with books I had amassed over the years. As I watched the students looking up and down the shelves, I remembered being a college student myself, awed by the bookshelves of my teachers. I had grown up in a house with lots of books, so it wasn't simply the presence of many books that impressed me. It was more that I wanted to know *which* books were on these shelves. I wanted to know what had made these professors into who they were, particularly the women. (Still today, I can name these women easily: Mary Gordon, Celeste Schenck, Timea Szell, Ann Lake Prescott, Nancy Stepan, Barbara Stoler Miller, Helene Foley.)

When my students looked at my bookshelves, I did not know what they saw. Perhaps for some it was simply a kind of wallpaper that attested to my expertise and my authority to teach them. Maybe to others, the sheer quantity explained my passion for the work I did.

But when I looked at my bookshelves, I saw my whole life: the "narrated 'I'" and the "narrating 'I,'" the various other homes these books had been, places they had lain undisturbed in cartons because I had no space to unpack them. It is my habit to leave receipts inside books, so I can recall where and when I bought them. In many cases, I could remember the interiors of those bookstores and where I had been living and with whom I had discussed these books, whether I had loaned them, and where I had sat reading them. On buses and subways and trains, in parks and at beaches, at tables in august university libraries with old reading lamps, and on lumpy couches at small cafes that have mostly since disappeared. I could reconstruct who had been my best friends, what streets I had walked daily, even what foods I had been in the habit of eating and what perfumes I had worn.

I looked at the thick purple spine of Anna Akhmatova's poetry; the yellow spine of the volume holding the letters exchanged between the legendary editor of children's books, Ursula Nordstrom, and her authors; the slim black volume with its hot pink title, *Only Words,* the manifesto of legal scholar Catherine MacKinnon; the Penguin Classic editions of ancient Chinese thought; the section of American history texts; the feminist studies on girls and their bodies; texts on women and class; the many editions of Shakespeare's works; and the well-worn nineteenth-century novels. It really was a mishmash. But at some point between childhood and now, I had brought these books together in their bodies and in my reading mind. I had studied, and teachers had invested in me. My parents had helped me find such teachers. They themselves had been my first such teachers, and now I wrote books. Now I taught students in a university; now I had three beautiful children of my own, a husband who loved me and also treated me well, and a house that I owned ("the bank owns it," my daughter liked to say after we explained to her how people buy houses), and a life. A whole life. A middle-class life in the United States, with more security than most, and lots of pleasure in my work. That was what my bookshelves had to say.

And that knowledge, too, was inseparable from my purpose as I sat with these students, one by one, and we worked on their essays. I sought to pinpoint the spots where a writer was not saying all he or she could and where they were avoiding saying things that would upset the cart, the sorts of things that would make it impossible to go back and end neatly. My English teacher in high school, an eccentric, demanding, creative woman with wild white hair, had told us never to write like we were working for Hallmark greeting cards. This came back to me now. And gently, very gently, I asked about the essays.

Now the language of "boring" was gone, for now it was personal, not abstract, and "boring" was hurtful. The collective humor of the classroom setting was gone and we sat at my desk, one-on-one, with a job to do.

"Your reader wants to know," I said, "if it was ever *hard* for the narrator to be the brother of an autistic sister, as much as he loved her. There is a point in your story when the parents say they need to take her to a special school and the narrator doesn't say anything back to them. It leaves the reader wondering what he was doing when they took her. Who took care of him, for instance?"

I said, "Dillon, look, I know the thing the narrator most wanted to be was an Eagle Scout, and I am sure that your dad was incredibly proud of him when he became one. But why did he leave the house the morning he got a phone call about it? Why did he go out to the pier by himself?"

"Maria, do you *like* the narrator who is fifteen when her dad loses her job?"

"James, why would a reader want to know about the fact that the narrator started to study harder after his mom told him to?"

Gentle pushes, prods, questions. I was authentically curious and so I wanted them to be curious.

I got some beautiful essays in the end. One young man wrote about fearing his grandfather and then discovering that his grandfather had feared him. A young woman thought back four years to realize that she had not understood why her father continued to spend money freely when he had lost his job and now understood that every time she held back when she wanted to buy something, she was trying to help the father who had disap-

pointed her. Another student had set out to please his father without knowing how and confessed that he still did not know. (Many fathers occupied
central roles in these essays.) A student who had been an Eagle Scout described
how he had loved earning badges through the tasks and challenges that others
assigned him. When it came time to earn his last badge, he was told that it
required an independent project. For a long time, he could not think of anything until, at the very last minute, it dawned on him that he wanted to plant
a flower garden in memory of a friend he had lost.

Human stories were pouring out of these kids in varying degrees of proficiency, but they were moving stories. Stories that moved me and stories
that themselves moved with each retelling. One young woman told me that
she was going to give her father the essay she had written as a gift. Another
student told me it was the most honest thing he'd ever written and that he
didn't know how it had come out of him but that he would save it. He did
not want to show it to anyone, but maybe someday he would.

Not every student had such an epiphany, but in this class that I saw as full
of particularly lovely and serious students, maybe fifteen out of twenty had fully
used the opportunity to work with me—an invested and skilled adult—and
come out with something that mattered to them.

BETWEEN HIGH SCHOOL AND COLLEGE:
JERUSALEM, 1988–1989

My students had come to the college classroom directly from high school.
In this way, their experience differed from mine. After a thirteen-year education in Jewish day schools, I had graduated in June 1988 from an Orthodox
high school in Chicago that encouraged its graduates to take a precollege
year to study in seminary in Israel. Seminary was single-sex, devoted to studying Jewish texts with partners and in classes, from the Five Books of Moses
and its commentaries, through the Talmud, to medieval and early modern
philosophy, to Hasidic thought, to contemporary explorations of Jewish
questions.[16]

I was one of eighty or so girls from across the United States and from
Australia, England, South Africa, and France who gathered in Jerusalem late
in August and set up apartments that would be our homes for the ten
months that followed. We slept, ate, prayed, and studied in the same building.

We encountered learned teachers who devoted their lives to our sacred texts and the communities of study built around them. Some of these women and men had been born in Israel, but many had emigrated from other places, seeing Israel as the center of the Jewish world, the place where Jewish history was happening—where the words of Torah were spoken in the streets and the Hebrew language was reinventing itself every day, where a once-in-two-thousand-year miracle was taking place—and they couldn't bear to keep far away. They were not fanatics of any sort. They were thoughtful, passionate people who wanted a hand in shaping contemporary Jewish sovereignty in the land of Israel.

Their politics ranged across the spectrum, but they were united in a love for the Jewish people, a love for the land, a love of Torah and God. They were not the ultra- Orthodox, who attempted to preserve a centuries-old Eastern European brand of Jewish life in Israel. They were modern men and women, almost all university educated, who sought to bridge the wisdom of the secular world with the light of Torah.

At eighteen, I saw in these teachers, and in many of the other Israelis I encountered, people whose lives were sanctified, burnished. American Jewry had never looked so impoverished to me as it looked that year from the vantage point of religious Jerusalem. The American Jewish middle class appeared committed to consuming—and consuming itself—with what George Eliot had called, "light fuel."[17]

What difficulties were there? Everything was available in the American marketplace and everyplace was the marketplace. Everything was light when I wanted only weighty.

At eighteen, what did I want? I wanted a world of high drama, of consequence, of purifying difficulty. I did not want a world where, on Sundays, people slept late, lounged in front of the television or wandered through the mall eating fast food, and buying, buying, buying. Ephemera. At eighteen, I wanted, more than anything, to serve what George Eliot called, "some object which would never justify weariness, which would reconcile self-despair with the rapturous consciousness of life beyond self." "Soul-hunger," Eliot named it, a voluntary submission to that which would transfigure our lives: "There would be nothing trivial about our lives. Every-day things with us would mean the greatest things."[18]

I didn't yet know the novels of George Eliot—the Victorian evangelical turned humanist storyteller—and, ironically, would only come to know them as a college student in the early 1990s. Eventually, I would recognize her as the single best describer of the passions of my early adulthood.

I wanted a life without days off, without moments off. I courted obligation. I couldn't understand the American Jewish lives I saw in Chicago's suburbs, where "American" dominated and "Jewish" seemed nothing but an easy overlay, to be assumed or removed when convenient. What kind of Judaism was it where the best and brightest went to business school or law school; where off-hours were spent playing sports or following high-paid teams; where the moment one returned from school, one slipped out of the dictated modest dress into clothes that reflected nothing but teen-America's most recent whim?

The Torah we learned was not merely a set of texts to study; these were the books of a lifetime and of eternity. The Torah was a holy aim that was impossible to achieve and vital to pursue. It made knowledge and goodness inseparable. There was no forgetfulness before God, and other people's lives were as sacred as our own.

In this heat, I studied Torah—and Israel—all year, and by springtime 1989, I was convinced that college was not the place for me. New York City was not the place for me. I would stay in Jerusalem. I would make my life there, where everyday things would mean the greatest things.

But then, in the most everyday way, my parents recalled me, quite simply, to the United States. I would, in the end, go to college. I would live in New York. I would study with the Centennial Scholars, with anthropologists and linguists and Talmudists and novelists and historians. I would see the homeless.

Instead of learning Torah in Jerusalem's houses of study, I would read George Eliot on the MTA and the Long Island Railroad, and I would come to recognize the wisdom and the hunger, the demands and the overwhelming plenty of America, of the university, of the English language.

It would not be easy.

BEIT RABBAN, JUNE 1993

As we study buildings, our minds turn to the wider subject of "homes." In 1993, the year I graduated from Barnard, Rudy Giuliani was elected mayor of New York City on the platform of improving the quality of life for New

Yorkers. He redescribed drunks, panhandlers, squeegee men, and peddlers as the "taxes" paid by law-abiding citizens of the city in the postrecession years. They were nothing but a blot on our vision and experience—an impediment to our pursuit of happiness. As he took office, the numbers of homeless one saw daily diminished notably, forcing the question of where they had all gone.

Still, in mid-1993, the Upper West Side numbered many homeless. On 86th Street and Columbus Avenue, sometimes Amsterdam, there was regularly a gray-haired man in jeans on the street corner by the diner. I passed him nearly every day, as did most of the Beit Rabban students. We passed him the day we went out observing the architecture of the neighborhood, and we passed him at times on the way to or from Central Park. Many of the kids knew him by name and waved or said hello. He was homeless.

Early in the year, the students had constructed a container to collect the coins of *tzedaka* they brought each Friday. We tried to allocate it monthly but in this case, a few months had gone by. Now, near the end of the year, we piled it up in pennies, nickels, dimes, and quarters, and worked together to count it. It amounted to about forty dollars. When we raised the question of allocation, the majority of the kids thought immediately of taking it to Andy on the corner.

Collecting money was only one part of the school's community service program. Each week, we sat together on the rug, and children and teachers would raise concerns about things they saw in the world or things we saw in the world that needed our attention. Together we cultivated the habit of noticing where help was needed—our help.

Community service with kids is a sensitive thing. It unfolds in live time, right here where we are; there is less of a protective buffer than in other forms of study. And what community service concerns most often is suffering and trouble. It focuses on things that should really be otherwise, that aren't fair or aren't just, or are simply very sad.

If you are a kid who comes from a community that stresses our responsibilities to others, you are likely to spot such trouble in the world fairly quickly. This is doubly true if you are a city kid, especially one who has been allowed and encouraged to notice rather than ignore or sidestep what surrounds him or her. And once you see what is before you, whether you are a child or an adult, it is at times natural to be drawn into despair, listlessness, fear, even terror.

Sitting together on the rug, and in discussion with Devora, I learned that the job was twofold: to help children see and feel the palpable claims upon us, which meant sometimes feeling sad and confused, and at the same time, to see and to feel that we could do something meaningful to help, which meant cultivating a sense of purpose and energy, and putting our minds to work creatively.

To cultivate such energy was much easier in company. We had each other. But we were not alone either. We joined forces with other organizations that were already working in the city and helped them a few times a year: we made cards, packed packages, and worked with seniors at Project Dorot for the elderly (where I also volunteered weekly throughout my college education); we visited the Jewish Home and Hospital and sang with its residents; we learned about Project ORE for poor, homeless, and mentally ill Jews; and met with kids from a school for the blind.

We had visitors come to talk with us about the work they were doing in the community. One man had founded an organization called New York Cares, and he came and sat in our classroom on a chair much too small for his long legs, and asked the kids, with all the kindness in the world, to think about what homeless people need. What would it be like to live between places, not to have a place to call home? He described a coat drive he ran yearly before the winter set in and the work of collecting coats: deciding where in the city to place containers, how to gather and sort the donations, and how to distribute the coats. I remember one child asking about how homeless people would take care of their teeth because where would they keep their toothbrushes? I remember discussing the problem of food because it is much more expensive to buy food already prepared, like a sandwich or a hot meal. Homeless people don't have a kitchen where they can store containers or a loaf of bread and utensils to prepare their own food, so how can they afford to keep eating? And where do they wash their hands if they get messy while eating?

Meeting that tall, gentle man from New York Cares prompted many practical ideas among the kids, including a book drive they organized the next year for a homeless shelter. Didn't homeless people need books too?

But I remember thinking, beyond the immediate outcome of our meeting, that now the possibilities for what one could be when one grew up had just expanded to include "founder of a volunteer association." Fireman, ballerina, teacher, lawyer, doctor . . . community service organizer.

And I remember thinking as I considered this circle of children that perhaps you find yourself wanting to take on such work later in life because you have tried to imagine how hard it is to be homeless and then, finding that imagination takes you only so far, you have actually investigated it, and then you have an idea of both its trials and of what it might take to limit or obviate them. Maybe you take on such work because in your experiment of wondering what it feels like to be homeless or through your investigation, you realize that the person who is homeless is not only homeless, but is also a person. Maybe you feel the energy to take on such work because you know that people are not only the condition in which they find themselves but possess reserves untapped and often undetected. They are more than homeless or hungry. Maybe you enter such work or maybe you find time for volunteering even if you have other work because when you were a child, the adults around you suggested that they would help you. Maybe you take on such work, part-time or full-time, because your education has reflected to you a respect for all human beings that is acted out in the everyday life of your classroom.

The ways you are taught to listen and speak to others no matter who they are, what they look like, where they come from, how they speak. The ways you are taught to ask about what you don't know, to recognize *that* you don't know, to look to others and to books or other sources to learn more. You feel a need to investigate. Your teachers help you cultivate the tendency to see both evident and unexpected connections, and to respond to what you have found or made with the desire to deepen or improve it.

Every day in school, you see and accept as natural that kids learn at different paces and in different ways.[19] Competition, self-defeat or self-congratulations ideally beside the point, a distraction from the real tasks at hand.

What you need, and what your teachers want to help you find, is the poise to go about your own work independently, with purpose, interest, and hope. Your own work goes on with or alongside others and you help them when they need it or seek their help when you need it. And always, always, there is the reality that the learning one does in school exceeds school; it concerns the world beyond the classroom. The learning one does outside of school can be brought back in, tested, affirmed, and refined in the company of teachers and friends.

These assumptions and the practices they give rise to are the infrastructure of learning, that is, the "building" and "home" of the kind of learning that might improve our world. This is the kind of learning that might help shape a human being who, we have reason to hope, will look beyond him- or herself.

Here, in a small classroom in New York City, we have tried to convey these beliefs to a group of young children. But I know, and later I see it proven true, that these beliefs and the practices they give rise to can inform a much larger classroom and can speak to older students, too. To be respected, to respect: so much comes from this.

MICHIGAN STATE UNIVERSITY, 2011

After the work of personal essays, we moved to our next subunit, education and truth telling. We had hit the point in the semester when I could see to the end of the term and my experience suggested that I could breathe a bit more easily, having done much of the heavy lifting for the course during its first half.

Over the summer, I had decided to open this section of the course with *The Trouble with Diversity* (2007), by Walter Benn Michaels, an iconoclastic professor of American literature.[20] In the late 1990s, I had heard him speak at a conference on the subject of this book. He was convinced then that Americans had taken up the banner of *cultural* diversity because of what it allowed us to sideline: *economic* diversity.

Cultural diversity, he argued, asked us only to grant that various forms of culture were equally worthy and should thus be nurtured and appreciated. But "economic diversity"? Those were actually fancy words for rich and poor. And it was enormously difficult to argue that being rich and being poor were equally good platforms for self-appreciation. What poor person wants to stay poor? What rich person does not want to remain rich? Economic diversity was nothing but inequality. And acknowledging inequality, not to mention acknowledging actual poverty, demanded action that many Americans were not eager to take.

I always debate hard before assigning a book because any book I assign means another will not get taught. As I reread Michaels, his tone was glib for my taste. And some of his claims were clearly contestable. Yet funda-mentally, Michaels presented himself as telling an inconvenient truth about the American unwillingness to confront economic inequality and about the limitations entrenched by poverty within our own borders.

Given the course's theme, I thought this rhetorical stance was notable. Given the course's aims, I appreciated the way the complex argument would train my students' minds. I thought they should learn how to read a cultural analysis that was not made in bullet points and that they might benefit from learning where universities and public intellectuals entered into conversations of national import. Finally, I thought students might learn from Michaels the value of critical introspection, since his book offered a critique of the Left not from the Right, but from within the Left.

If Michaels had created something of a storm in the wake of his speech at the small conference at the end of the 1990s, it was nothing compared to the reaction he evoked in my classroom full of students born in 1992 or 1993, high school graduates in 2011.

They hated his book. They didn't understand it; they hadn't read it care-fully, but they hated it. They detested his argument (I wondered whether it should even be construed as an argument given that it was so patently a fact) that rich kids were more likely to succeed in this country than poor kids.

Specifically, they rejected outright the idea that how much money you had—that is, how much money your parents had—affected the education and thus the future that the United States offered you. My students believed that the ideal of equal opportunity in education was an achieved reality in the United States. They believed the nation was a meritocracy. If students got into good colleges, this proved that they were smarter or had worked harder than those who had not gotten in. They believed this to be true with-out respect to any outside factors.

Especially outrageous to my students was a small point about seventy pages into the short book where Michaels had suggested that if we, as Americans, were truly committed to equal opportunity in education, we would not link property taxes to the funding of neighborhood public schools. Laser-like, the students returned to this again and again in our opening dis-cussion (perhaps unaware that twenty years earlier, Michigan had passed Proposition A, seeking to disconnect property taxes from public school funding and, in principle at least, succeeding).

"You can throw as much money as you want at the problem," said Kate, "but you know that in the end, it's not about dollars. Those people need to be willing to work harder. They don't really want to succeed."

My ears rang from the "those people," but before I could ask any probing questions, Dillon offered his view: "Anyway, the federal government makes up the difference between the taxes in different areas. It's pretty equal in the end. And did you know that in some schools that get more money per kid, the kids still don't do well?"

"This is an insulting argument. My father's dad came from Ireland and he taught my dad to work hard. They had barely any money and my dad still succeeded at school and in life."

One after the next offered a version of "It's not about money."

I tried to suggest that poverty was real, that it made a difference to the offerings of different schools. Nobody bit.

"There's always going to be poverty, it doesn't matter what anyone does to help," one student commented.

I felt I had absolutely no idea where this conversation was going or even what we were really talking about. It was the sort of unhinged discussion I was utterly unused to having in my classroom: a kind of free-for-all, detached from any text. These "arguments" were based on pure opinion and force of feeling. This was the sort of discussion I rejected out of hand as inappropriate for the kindergarten classroom, let alone the university. Yet here we were. Here I was.

"Would it be a better world if there weren't poverty?" I asked in the purest hypothetical I could come up with. Its answer seemed obvious to me, something we could all agree on.

"Hierarchy is inevitable."

"If no one is poor, then the least rich will feel poor."

"It's all relative."

I insisted on my thought experiment: "But wouldn't it be better if there were some minimal standard that all people lived above?"

I wasn't getting any takers on this question, which would commit them to nothing. As I stood at the front of the room, leaning on the table that held my books, I took in the situation. Clearly, many of my students' political positions differed from my own. I would not have guessed their views on domestic politics based on their willingness to consider the critique of American violence and global intervention that we had seen in *Jarhead*. But

I had had many students over the years with whom I differed politically. I knew this because of things they said rather than things I said. I felt keenly the responsibility not to address politics in the language of contemporary news, though ethics could never stay out of the humanities classroom if serious learning were going on. But when you teach in the wake of 9/11 and Hurricane Katrina, and through four presidential elections, campaigns on campus, and two wars, you can often gauge generally where your students stand, just as they can often gauge where their professors stand.

So it wasn't the fact that many of them were probably avid Republicans or that they were against affirmative action and possibly against taxes in general that disturbed me. A difference in views was the norm. It wasn't a certain tone and an offensiveness in certain comments that was bothering me. No professor teaches for nearly two decades without managing their share of offense. Once, a student at a different university had asked me why Jews couldn't just get over the Holocaust already.

But the day we discussed Michaels, I felt like I was on a sinking ship. I stood at the front of the classroom and listened to twenty eighteen- and nineteen-year-olds talk back to a book a hundred times more tricky than they imagined it to be that was motivated from a political position they could not actually identify and argued in terms that they had not yet strived to comprehend. Their beliefs were so strong: their beliefs in themselves, in their idea of the United States, in their parents' political convictions. And their knowledge of the world was so limited. What confidence they had!

As a group, they appeared to reject a version of the "blank slate" notion that, to me, has always been profoundly moving. Education, I have believed, is offered to the blameless young: to those who have not yet made or squandered choices that their parents and grandparents were offered. What can equal opportunity mean but precisely this disproportionate relation between personal future and past: a long future ahead, a short past behind? Promise. Freedom.

I found that I was actually losing my breath. I felt a strong, sudden, and unfamiliar urge to seize every ounce of authority my position vested in me and shut them up. End this stupidity. Tell them the real facts, mock them for their naïveté and their small-world insularity. Mock the backwater towns and awful suburbs they came from and their parents, who were less educated than I. I was filled with hatred, there at the front of the classroom, and the force of the hatred was also what was taking my breath from me.

A student I had liked so much, David, the one who wrote about his grandfather in his essay, slouched in his seat, obviously unaware of my distress, and offered the following: "Anyway, these stories aren't our stories. We all got in here. So why should we care?"

My mind nearly exploded. It wasn't the ungenerosity of this thought. I could imagine a student *thinking* it to him- or herself. I just couldn't imagine him or her *saying* it out loud.

I thought of the hours upon hours I had put into reading their personal essays, including David's excellent essay. I thought about how I had been happy to give each of the students my help and to seek their advancement, well-being, and growth. And I felt the force of their indifference to the poor, not just the adult poor, but poor children and teenagers who did not have their opportunities.

At the front of the room, I felt combative, polemical, angry, outraged, and indignant, all the bad things that do not help people teach effectively or speak from the heart in a way that might enter another's heart. A teacher of mine had once taught me a rabbinic saying that translates roughly as follows: "Set words upon the heart and maybe it will open up and the words will fall in."

This peace was eluding me and so for a minute I began to argue. I don't recall what I said. Then I got momentarily wise and shut up, and let my students take hold of the discussion. Almost always a better strategy in such circumstances.

A young woman whom I knew to have grown up in an evangelical household replied to David, "Well, there's a moral reason to care."

But that didn't go anywhere. It simply fell out of the discussion and she didn't even seem to believe it that much herself.

David unslouched long enough to reconsider briefly and said, "I guess it's not good if your district has to pay for crime costs that grow out of a permanent underclass."

Fair enough, the self-interest argument. But all that was making itself available to me in the silent argument going on in my head was the language of justice. All right, if morality, compassion, and empathy had no claim on these students, then what about the great American values of fairness, equity, justice?

In other words, "This isn't right because it's not fair and thus it is your business as an American who would like the country to reflect its stated ideology just the least bit."

I made this suggestion out loud and it fell flat.

Finally, Rob, a student whom I always thought of as a "nice young man"—blond and tall, he'd had a prominent deformity as a child that had altered the nature of his own school experience (I knew this because of their personal essays)—returned to the language of compassion.

"My mother is a teacher," he said, "and she told me that there are schools that are *really* in bad shape. I think it would be hard to do well in those kinds of schools, even if you are trying, like, really hard. I mean, how can you learn if you don't have the books you need or the class is enormous?"

Our sole African American student, a young woman who had struggled with multiple sclerosis, said, "Well, in my school, there was not always toilet paper in the bathrooms and other necessities." A voice of wake-up, a reality check.

When I said, teachers spend their own money to bring school supplies in places where there simply are none, Kate said, "Well, why should schools be providing those things to begin with?"

I jumped in, again trying to find a baseline.

"Are there some things we can assert about public schooling: for instance, every student should have a chair? Or, in the winter, there should be heat?"

I got my first grudging universal yes to this. Yes, there should be heat.

"I hear those of you who are saying that 'throwing money at the problem won't solve it,' but can we not agree that without money, some problems *cannot* be solved? That money is a necessary if not sufficient piece of the solution?"

There was a pause.

"I mean, if your school is too cold to learn in, like hypothermia cold, you can't make it warm just by having a good enough attitude, can you?"

I felt us falling off reality into an America where schooling was not a citizen's right at all.

Dirk interrupted my silent reverie.

"The 'poor' people they're talking about in the book, you know?" his fingers quoted in the air, "in their culture, they don't want to work hard, they don't value education."

I could only assume that "their culture" meant blacks. I suppose it could also have meant Latinos. Maybe poor whites.

Provoked despite myself, I said, "Really? Wouldn't you assume that if someone *is* poor, they'd have a lot of reason to want to be *not* poor? Wouldn't you think that education would be something that at least *some* of 'them' would have reason to desire very strongly? At least for their kids?"

Silence.

There was so much more to be said: how difficult it is to assess the choices people make, from the nearly miraculous choices for the good, to choices that seem almost calculated to work against long-term self-interest. These are choices that are constrained in ways that outsiders can barely imagine— choices that don't look at all like choices to the people making them.

There in my classroom, if we were to do these questions justice, there was history to be considered, at least three centuries worth. There were governmental policies, federal laws, public health provisions, urban demographics, moral philosophy, developmental psychology, brain science. How difficult and insoluble so much of this was. I shrank from all I could not understand or integrate.

But class was still unfolding.

"Well," said Dirk, "I don't know why I think this, I mean I don't have any evidence, but I'm going to say it anyway—"

I jumped in before he could commit himself: "Are you sure you want to?"

"Yes," he said.

I don't remember what he said next, because for me it did not matter. The class session turned on that "yes," the essence of privilege. (Later, I would reconsider and wonder if it were not ignorance and immaturity on its way to hardening into culpable assumption of privilege. Here was my task: to check it.)

I had designed my classroom to be a place for questions and trying out possible answers and measuring them against all the various forms of data we could gather. But I needed partners.

If a student could boldly demonstrate in a college classroom before his or her professor and classmates this untroubled ability to deflect information and to posit a position as true just because one wished it so, what were the chances for public discourse? What would be the fate of American truth telling after all?

◆ ◆ ◆

The rest of the day went by in a blur. I felt physically ill from what had transpired and the truth I had been forced to confront in my classroom.

Ori picked me up at five o'clock since he too was teaching that semester at MSU, as a visiting faculty member in the English department. I fell into the car. I felt I had been betrayed, though I knew immediately in the hollow pit of my stomach that I had presumed too much: too much kinship, the sense of a shared endeavor. I had been taken in by the all-too-common misconception of the teacher that the students are as invested as you are, that the work you are doing together takes up as much psychic space for them as it does for you.

But most of all, I had presumed a shared ethics of compassion, not a politics but a simple ethics, undetailed in its mechanics, but fundamental. An ethics that motivated the care with which I had read their essays and the faith with which I came to work.

I told Ori what had happened.

"Republican talking points," he said. "That's all you're dealing with."

Sure, I could hear that, too. I imagined that these first-year students had been repeating what they had heard around the dinner table in recent years, especially in the wake of the Michigan debates on affirmative action. But it cut so close to the bone for me. What I wanted at that moment was actually to quit my job. I wanted to go home, wherever home might be: to a community of people who knew that compassion was absolute and necessary, who believed as I did that the aim of human life was to collect the sparks, to transform, and to make holy. I wanted to be in the company of people who believed that no world where some people suffered because they were poor or black or both was a good enough world. I wanted to roll up my sleeves and go work somewhere where I could understand why I was taking time away from my own children to give to someone else's.

I sunk deeper into the front seat and turned off the radio.

Ori said, "Hey, don't give up. Take it is an opportunity; you have the chance to get these kids to think new thoughts, to learn stuff they've never been exposed to. You're the other voice."

Everything he said was true, but none of it seemed to matter enough. I wasn't ready yet to think rationally about what role I could play, how I might start from a different set of assumptions in the classroom and work forward. When I think of it now, I know that what I was doing was mourning. I was mourning my idea of some of those students; I had seen a new, rougher side of them and I could not yet incorporate it into the rest of what I knew about them. I couldn't read it back into our work on their essays or their openness and curiosity about matters that threatened them less. But even more than these particular students, I was mourning a certain alliance with my own work, a fit I had not needed to question because it was self-evident. I had held an idea of what it was I was doing with my time, my skills, my life, an idea that now seemed unmerited. Had it always been a figment of my imagination?

We arrived home and our babysitter, Lori, who was watching Tzipora and Priya, looked at me and asked, "Wow, did you have a hard day? You don't look too good."

I said to her and mainly to Priya, who looked immediately worried, "Some of my students said things today that were really upsetting."

"Like what?" Priya asked.

So I said, "Well, one student said that if other people don't have the things they need to learn and to be healthy, why should I care?"

Priya looked at me, mouth agape: "He said that?"

"He did."

In the car, I had said to Ori, "If my child said such a thing, I would believe I had failed utterly as a parent."

Priya's face and voice, Tzipora's dense little body, Lori's relation to us, Ori, Shai, the space of our house: all these things brought me back home. Here was where the work lay. Here, we would build something that mattered and that traveled from inside our home to outside, something that would characterize our whole lives, that we couldn't set down for a minute.

BEIT RABBAN, READING-WRITING WORKSHOP

During the early 1990s, I spend an unusual amount of time and money in the excellent children's bookstores of the Upper West Side, browsing among mothers with strollers and far more seasoned teachers. Although I am twenty-three and not yet a parent, I have a good sense for children's books, honed by a mother who bought, borrowed, and read us the best stories she could find. I love picture books because of all the books I own, they are the only ones likely to be reread and enjoyed hundreds of times.

My most recent acquisition is a new book, still available only in hard-cover but worth the expense: *Peppe the Lamplighter*, by Elisa Bartone, illus-trated by Ted Lewin, a Caldecott Honor Book. When I bought picture books in those days, I had the Beit Rabban kids in mind, but somewhere, too, I was thinking of my own future, a family I could not yet imagine.

I bring the book to school the next day and set it out in the morning for kids to look at in their free time. When reading-writing workshop time came, I pick it up and we gather in a circle on the rug.

I never ignore the covers of picture books, though I can still hear my grandmother's voice telling me, "don't judge a book by its cover." I am sure they will want to talk about the golden, raised Caldecott sticker because we have studied this award and considered what makes a book "good."

But when I ask what they notice, Rachel raises her hand to say that she sees a boy lighting a lamp with a stick instead of turning a switch, and that this probably means the story took place a long time ago. Ari says there could be a button on the stick and so maybe it is more recent, but as soon as we begin to read, there is no question: "A long time ago when there was no electricity and the streetlamps in Little Italy had to be lit by hand, Peppe lived in a tenement on Mulberry Street."

The silence in the room is my invitation. Everyone is listening. I read the story through, without explaining or asking anything; I hate the idea of interrupting the rhythm. Explanations and clarifications can come later.

Now, my eyes move from the page to the children's faces, back and forth in the kind of automatic movement that is itself a learned rhythm. I show the pictures, giving them plenty of time to see. When we read, I am glad for the intimacy of the classroom because my emotion runs high. Good stories can do so much. I feel a welcome pressure of performance, and also joy: when I read aloud, watch their faces, and hear my own voice in the other-wise silent room, I feel like I am in exactly the right place.

When I am done reading, the room holds its stillness for an extra moment. Where to begin with this tale of a motherless boy and his many sisters, his desire for a job to help the family he loves, the father's anger that his son wants to work on the streets, lighting the lamps, when he has brought him to America for better things? And the fateful, dark night when little Assunta does not come home and the father begs Peppe to light the lamps. The reunion of brother and sister, then the father's pride in his son who lights each lamp, imagining it to be a "small flame of promise for the future," and Assunta's love for Peppe, who has "the best job in America": scaring the dark away.

I am still absorbed by Peppe's prayers and Assunta's fears, and by the chiaroscuro illustrations that use the light and dark to illuminate the faces of the brother and the sister as they find each other.

"It was the olden days," says Rachel, breaking my reverie.

"Like American Girl times."

We talk about what a century is, and how this story is set at the turn of the twentieth century, about one hundred years earlier. But then the conversation takes a turn. What really interests lots of kids is the question of where this story takes place.

"They're in Italy," says Masha, but Zach says, "No, *Little* Italy. Italy is across the Atlantic Ocean, but Little Italy isn't. Remember, the man goes back to Italy to get his wife and that's why Peppe is lighting the lamps for him?"

We get the globe. We point to Italy. We point to where we are. We note the ocean in between.

"So where does this story happen?" I ask.

"It's in America!" Ari proclaims, "because the father says, 'I didn't bring my family to America for my son to be on the street.'"

We find the page where the father says that. Already these kids have learned that answers require evidence.

"So how is Peppe in Little Italy and America at the same time?"
Silence.

I tell them that Little Italy is actually a place in America, and not only that, it's in New York, like we are. It's a neighborhood downtown.

"You could take the subway there," I say.

Victoria raises her hand and says her friend Luca just moved back to Italy and she is going to e-mail with him. (Victoria is on the cutting edge and explains what e-mail is, this being the early 1990s.)

"Right, because Italy is really far from New York, too far for a play date."

"I could take a plane to the play date," she says and laughs out loud.

Back to Little Italy, I ask the kids who they think might live in Little Italy in New York, and someone suggests that it is people from the big Italy.

I tell them that sometimes when people leave the country they live in, they like to settle in a new place with people they already know, with friends and family.

Hannah raises her hand. "They probably missed the big Italy, so they wanted all to live in one place, which was like a little Italy, and make it look like the place they left."

Though she has stopped talking, she looks as if she has not finished thinking. I pause.

"It would be more 'home-ish' that way," she concludes.

"I think it's like Chinatown," says Zach.

Together, a few kids describe what they imagine: that people from China made a town that seemed like China, where people ate food that came from China and lived with other Chinese friends and talked and wrote in Chinese.

"So," I say, "what language do you think Peppe and his family might be speaking in Little Italy?"

One of the children calls out, "Italian!"

I turn to the page where Peppe's father discovers that Assunta is lost and asks, "Dov'e mia bambina?"

I read the sentence aloud, along with the sentence in English preceding it, and then the one succeeding it: "Assunta would always be Papa's baby."

"I'm wondering what you think the father is saying," I say, and a child immediately says, "I miss my baby."

"Right, very close. You know," I say, "I actually looked it up and it means, where is my baby? *Dov'e mia bambina?*"

I reread the three sentences.

"I wonder why the author would have written that sentence in Italian when the whole rest of the book is in English, especially since probably not everyone will understand it."

Batsheva says, "Maybe he didn't know how to say that sentence in English."

"The author or the father?" I ask Batsheva.

Another child says there are other words in Italian in the story but that the author definitely knows lots of English. The author knows two languages but maybe the dad in the story only knows Italian because he was born in the big Italy and only came to the United States when he was already grown up and wouldn't go to school.

I look at the kids and say: "You know what I just thought of? Maybe the whole story of the family and the neighborhood is happening in Italian but the author writes the story in English, kind of like she's translating all the conversations for us. That way even people who don't know Italian can understand the story."

"Then the Italian sentence is the only real sentence!" Zach says gleefully.

"I know what you mean," I say, "but explain it!"

And he does.

I go back to the page where all of Peppe's sisters are named: Angelina, Mariuccia, Assunta, Filomena.

"All those names are Italian," says one of the kids.

"It's a world in Italian," I say.

"Who here has a name that isn't originally English?"

Suddenly, they notice that many of the names in our classroom are Hebrew.

"It's Little Israel," says one of the kids, "because they talk Hebrew in Israel and we talk it here."

Then a child says, "I know a West Side Israel," and when I ask what it is, he says it is the shul, the synagogue, on his block.

"Maybe New York is made up of all kinds of 'little' places," I say. "When you go from one to the other, you can feel the difference because suddenly you'll hear a different language."

"Like Spanish!"

"Or Russian!"

Half an hour has gone by and we haven't talked at all about the plot of this story, ostensibly its main drama—the conflict and reconciliation of father and son, the child gone missing at night, then found. We haven't talked about what it means that Peppe's father doesn't want his son to work on the streets; I'm sure many kids did not understand that. Nor have we discussed the moment when Peppe lights the lamps, wishing something as each flame flares, and compares it to lighting candles in church. We haven't talked about when and why children look for work, for money.

So we will read this story again tomorrow. I know no one will object. And perhaps tomorrow I will be surprised again by what matters. Perhaps I will have my own plan for what matters.

But today, I have learned that some children divide stories into then and now, the olden days and today. I don't know what the implications of this divide are, but I now know it is one way they classify what they encounter.

I know we can look at many books through this prism and consider whether their stories could possibly travel through time: How important is it to this story that it is set when it is set? Could Victoria's image of a plane trip to Italy be inset here? How would the new mode of e-mail communication we have just learned about change this story? Could this story happen at all at a different moment in history? How can we tell in what era a story is set if there aren't pictures and the author does not tell us immediately? What differences can we find between a story *set* in the "olden days," and a story that was actually written and published in the "olden days"? How do writers writing today know what the olden days were like?

I have material here for weeks. We are talking about history and how it is transformed into literary matter. Someone is sure to ask about truth, and then another child will likely raise the possibility of realist fiction, and then if we want, we can be off and running for a few more weeks.

I know kids will want to write their own versions of all the sorts of texts we are describing, defining, and reading: stories set in other times and places; stories that move between languages to define cultural spaces; stories that merge now and then in zany, impossible ways. They will want to make lists of modern inventions that tell us that a story is set today, and lists of books published before the year a child was born, or before 1900 or some other watershed year that we can study (we can learn where to look for the publication year and some kids will focus, no doubt, on the numerical challenges of counting backward in four digits). We can write letters to historians or to writers of historical fiction, or to the founder of the American Girl doll company.

But it is not only the "olden days" and history that have come up this afternoon. The thing that held us longest in discussion was the idea of Little Italy. As I mull this finding later, I am moved by it, because they have hit on something so relevant to their own lives, as children, as Jews, as human beings for whom an undivided world is always too big. We need "little" spaces, organized by language, food, images, people, ideals. Little homes that do not shut out what surrounds but protect us from some of the harshest realities of the world beyond.

I have always thought of classrooms as such "little" spaces, where the teacher must work to invent a common language out of shared experience and study. The teacher works to create a culture of home that one can think back on later, as a place worth reproducing somewhere else, only bigger.

MICHIGAN STATE UNIVERSITY, 2011

The night after my difficult class session, I had sat at my computer, still stunned, and mulled my options. While I was considering, I checked with Ori, then made a $200 donation to the Children's Defense Fund. This was the equivalent of a month of Priya's twice-weekly after-school care. But maybe it could contribute to something meaningful somewhere else. Other people's children were no less precious to them than mine were to me. I had told my students that money was not sufficient, but that it was necessary. I had meant the state's money, but I had also meant our own.

Sitting there at my laptop, the site of much of my work as a researcher and writer, I knew I had to take a step back from my college students, who were indeed, not "my" students, but their own. I had been presuming too much and the only solution for either of us was for the students to get to work, a different and new kind of work that I would direct.

Whatever they believed about poverty, African Americans, themselves, the United States, affirmative action, or money, I was going to raise the intellectual bar. They would have to subordinate themselves to a set of logical ideas until they understood those ideas well enough to be qualified to speak about them. And so I assigned demanding essay questions that required that they reread *The Trouble with Diversity* from start to finish, represent its ideas in quotation, and only in the last instance respond to its ideas with their own questions and critiques. Opinion had taken the day in the first class session and I would see analysis replace it.

Then I revised the syllabus: first, we would read Jonathan Kozol, the well-known author of multiple exposés of the inequalities of American public education. I knew that there were journalists who argued that Kozol had done little independent research and that his work made his largely African American subjects into little more than victims of circumstances. But I also knew that when I had read *The Shame of the Nation* as a general audience member, the data and the stories in Kozol's book had been eye-opening. Maybe the reaction to Michaels in my classroom had been linked partially to the absence of personal stories in his argument. Michaels seemed a bit of a misanthrope, whereas Kozol was a defender of children.

One of my aims in teaching university students, particularly those from less cosmopolitan places in Michigan, was to bring scholars and artists to life, so I planned to screen a YouTube interview with Kozol after they had read chapters from his book. My students were all too likely to say "they" when referring to the author of a book because they did not seem to trace it back to an actual person who had done the labor of writing. I wanted them to begin substituting images of real thinkers for an anonymous corporate entity that demanded their attention and was somehow connected to the authorities who produced textbooks and also gave grades. I wanted them to join the intellectual cultural elite that need not be an elite.

Back in class, the students bridled at the return to Michaels, but they did the work. Because Michaels was a writer with style and not always predictable in his moves, they could barely tell when he was introducing a point with which he agreed or which he sought to criticize. In short, they were not especially capable readers of sophisticated prose and while this came as no surprise to me, now I found it newly depressing and troubling.

What if they didn't get to be better readers in college? What if they left in caps and gowns, with their diplomas and degrees, not much more capable than they had come in? What if all we were doing in college was offering window dressing to mediocre high school educations? What if the intellectual cultural elite couldn't be democratized? What if the policy minds we were supposedly training at this particular college would never ask questions that led to new or unexpected answers, but would remain at the level of vague and general understanding rather than becoming truly expert and nuanced?

Yet nuance and complexity could potentially stand in the way of action. Few literary scholars, for whom these were the disciplinary bywords, wrote books or articles with significant real-world effects. One of the things I liked about where I worked was that theory and practice, knowledge and action, were clearly intertwined. I had a chance to challenge students who planned to lead lives of public action.

Indeed, Kozol was eye-opening for many of my students, just as he had been for me. First of all, unlike Michaels, he was heroic in his way. He had gone into the schools, he had worked for and with kids, he had sat with them, talked, learned, investigated. He was sentimental and he was angry, a kind of Hebrew Bible prophet telling the truth as he saw it: perfect for our course.

But my students were impressed by something else, too: they noted that Kozol had gone to Harvard. If he had gone to Harvard, and then chosen a path with little glamour or power, maybe the problem he was describing was real. Why else would a person with every door open to him make such a choice? (Again, I had been blindsided: Harvard was a real place to me. I had friends who had studied there and friends who taught there; I had walked its squares. But for these students, it was uncharted territory, as much metaphor as was Hollywood or New York City or Paris. Neither did they realize that it is often precisely those students coming from Harvard who feel free to choose the less remunerative paths that might be impossible for others to elect.)

Kozol's argument was as simple as it was disturbing. He claimed that the United States today was more racially segregated than it had been in the era of the civil rights movement. In short, he said, we have gone backward as a nation instead of forward.

The idea that progress has failed is never a comfortable one. As much as it is a common conservative trope to argue for a return to founding ideals, it is also profoundly counter-American to suggest that we have gotten worse at anything truly consequential, that we aren't naturally perfecting our union. Progress, especially for people in their twenties, is an idea we feel in our bodies, as we get bigger, stronger, more able. Moral and intellectual progress seem simply a corollary.

With Kozol, some students began to wonder about their own opinions while others expressed shock, and some conveyed appreciation for new information.

"This is life changing," wrote one, "to read this stuff."

Sentimental hyperbole or the beginnings of a vocation? It was impossible to know in the moment.

When I told them that for their next assignment, they would investigate their own home public school districts or any private schools they had attended, many turned to the assignment with ready curiosity. By no means a statistician, I nonetheless wanted them to gather some data: I wanted to know numbers.

This was probably more unusual for me, a scholar of literature, than for them—students who had selected an undergraduate school focused on public policy. I asked them to find out how many students sat in classrooms. I wanted attendance rates, free lunch rates, ethnic percentages, scores on state and national exams, graduation rates. I wanted to know what extracurricular activities there were and what costs, if any, were associated with participating. What teams existed? How were they funded? What was the physical plant like? I also wanted to know about the online identity of the school: their websites and the technology in and around the school. I, too, investigated widely, spending hours at the computer, comparing schools across the state.

Back in the classroom, students sit in groups of three and report to each other on average income in their school districts and neighboring districts. When we return from groups to the full class circle, many students express surprise that the high schools that trained them have almost no (officially) poor kids or black or Latino kids.

I am reminded of my own surprise in the two years I served as a reader for the college's "diversity" scholarship at how few essays—maybe five or six—were written by students who were actually minority applicants while the rest, more than a hundred, were written by white students who had never experienced ethnic "diversity" and were seeking to come to MSU to learn about it. MSU was their big city, their entry into a world less homogenous than the places they had grown up, and yet, how homogenous it still was. The diversity scholarships were divided up among minority students and majority students just like themselves: those who wanted to encounter the "diverse."

My students report with less surprise what they already knew: that almost every student from their schools succeeds in graduating; many of them cite 98 percent. I inform them that in Michigan, "economically disadvantaged" students graduate high school at a rate of 64 percent. Some students report that schools mere minutes from where they live—the next district over—have drastically different populations and outcomes from their own districts.

A lone student from Illinois says it had never occurred to him to think about extracurricular offerings: he assumed all schools had them. At this point, I myself do not know enough to tell him that in Michigan's poorer and more dangerous cities, not all schools have recess, let alone extracurricular activities. At some of these schools, after second grade, kids do not go outside from 7 A.M. to 2:45 P.M. But even without that information, these freshmen are waking up to the truths of economic difference.

I have already shifted the syllabus around so much that I contemplate turning the rest of the semester into a seminar on public education in the United States. Except that it is not my field. I check the college's list of course offerings and am reassured to recall that we teach social theory and social relations, the civil rights movement and contemporary race relations, the history of childhood in America, and a seminar devoted in its entirety to access, affordability, and quality in higher education.

And so we give the subject one more week, screening the flawed but meaningful film *Waiting for Superman*. I ask them to find and analyze negative and positive reviews. They learn the name Diane Ravitch, the eminent historian of education who helped establish the infrastructure of No Child Left Behind, and then, remarkably, recanted publicly in a major book, in response to what she described as the policy's empirical failure. In these ways and a few others, the students enter into the national debate on public education (the education that shaped them) and the corporatization of schooling and testing.

When the week is done, I do not seek to wrap up our inquiry with any neat conclusions. In any event, the equilibrium that grounds me in the classroom—that I didn't even know grounded me in the classroom—is lost to me, and I am simply trying to pull through.

We return to the syllabus. We pick up with family and truth; then gender, sexuality, and truth. By the end of the semester, I can say unequivocally that no truth so collectively unsettled these students as the inequality of contemporary American education. This, to me, is an extraordinary finding. Disparity in educational opportunity is more disturbing and conflictual for this group of eighteen-year-old Middle Americans than a critique of their nation's military agenda; than the exposure of myths about our most intimate institution, the family; than the challenges of sexual identity.

School is at the very heart of who we are. Ideas can take an extraordinarily long time to germinate. Going back through my e-mails, I see that it has been three years since my senior colleagues at James Madison had invited me to give an informal talk as part of a series of faculty workshops in fall 2008. Instead of having taken the obvious path of presenting my work on ethics and economics in Victorian fiction, I had found myself preparing notes on the relations between reading, empathy, and action.[20]

I began with George Eliot, who had written the mid-nineteenth century's most famous recommendation of the moral force of art, claiming that novels could do more to extend human sympathies than any sermon or scholarly study. She argued that appeals "founded on generalizations and statistics require a sympathy ready-made, a moral sentiment already in activity."[21] By contrast, she asserted, "a picture of human life such as a great artist can give, surprises even the trivial and the selfish into that attention to what is apart from themselves, which may be called the raw material of moral sentiment."

For years, while writing my dissertation and then working on articles and my first scholarly monograph, I had mulled that passage. I read and reread Eliot's novels, which preached and exemplified the necessity of extending our imaginations so that we might understand not only the content of another person's perspective but absorb the challenging truth that each of us has an "equivalent centre of self, whence the lights and the shadows must always fall with a certain difference."[22]

It took me many years to realize what was missing from Eliot's doctrine of what she called sympathy and we call empathy: action. Eliot's doctrine glorified knowledge and feeling. Presumably, these capacities would lead to moral action of some kind, but typically in her novels, this action was subsumed within a very small scope, among one's own intimates. True, the famous essay on art and sympathy did discuss legislative action, but that was reserved for legislators. What was the ordinary person meant to do with the empathic knowledge cultivated by novel reading or art more generally? How might the extended imagination—specially attuned to the suffering of others—be put to use?

And further, how would the evolved reader diffuse the guilt and resentment that could come with the recognition of others' need and prevent action, rather than prompt it? How would that reader break through to a personal balance that would allow him or her to reach out to others—sometimes known, sometimes unknown—in compassion and identification? How would the identification elude condescension, presumption, falsity?

I had pressing questions about the theory, the novels, and the novelist that had come across my world twenty years earlier with such beauty and moral force. These questions about reading, empathy, and action seemed only to multiply the longer I taught literature.

Now it was 2011, three years after I had used that talk to investigate with my intelligent and receptive colleagues—almost none of whom taught humanities—the social meaning of teaching in the humanities. And here I was, facing what looked to me like the same questions.

I thought back to the many semesters I had taught literary texts that evoked the centuries-long ravages of American slavery and the systematic murder of the Holocaust. I recalled the students who had described their encounter with Toni Morrison or Charlotte Delbo or Primo Levi as shocking, eye-opening. But what did that shock amount to? What civic role did it play? How was I helping to funnel knowledge into meaningful living?

In an attempt to take this morally fraught course and make links between reading and living, I almost always assigned students Levi's provocative essay on the support that obscure language provided the rule of fascism; his argument transcended the rise of the Third Reich and cast us back on our own moment.[23] In the same vein, we often read an article by the astute cultural critic Jonathan Rosen arguing that an appropriate American response to the Holocaust was not imaginative identification with the victims (à la the Holocaust Museum in Washington) but an intensive education in democratic values.[24] These essays successfully brought us into the present tense. But to what end?

In 2001, a full decade earlier, I had asked a class of capable freshmen at the University of Michigan at the end of that uniquely intense and turbulent fall semester whether they imagined that their exposure to the course's texts would lead to any different behaviors in their lives.[25] I asked them to write their reflections anonymously and told them I was asking simply from curiosity, that it was unrelated to their academic performance in the course. I remember one student who wrote something like, "Honestly, no. It was disturbing when I read about the racism but I think it will fade as time passes." One or two wrote that they would read the newspaper more regularly; some wrote that they might look into causes on campus. Another wrote something like, "Since slavery is done, I don't think there is much to do on that." At least in that case, I hurriedly emended the syllabus to end the course with a film on modern slavery, to correct the historical mistake, and to clarify that work remained.

The following year I asked students to hand in with their final writing portfolios two newspaper articles (contemporary, not historical) that seemed to them connected to the course material. I had not been sure what I wanted them to do with these articles. I had had no idea how to use them in the classroom and so had simply included them in the final submission.

Ten years had passed and I was still debating what to do with the news, with today—with real life and politics, that difficult, cautionary word.

What is the link between thought and action? In *The Moral Life of Children*, Robert Coles observes that there is no necessary link: "A well-developed conscience does not translate, necessarily, into a morally courageous life. Nor do well-developed powers of philosophical thinking and moral analysis necessarily translate into an everyday willingness to face down the various evils of this world."[26] But then he poses the critical question: "What makes for a moral *life*—for moral *action*—as opposed to moral reflection and analysis and argument?" When we see what he calls "moral spirit" and "moral leadership," *where does it come from?*[27] I have always believed that it comes from homes and classrooms, of course, it comes also from youth groups, and religious or political organizations shaped by an educational mission.

But Coles looks for answers along a different axis, a historical one: "I believe that the active idealism we see in some of our young takes place . . . when a beckoning history offers, uncannily, a blend of memory and desire; a chance to struggle for a new situation that holds a large promise, while earning along the way the approval of one's parents, neighbors, friends, and, not least, oneself."[28] There are moments, he suggests, when the public and the private blend, and when a difficult but somehow fortifying past provides impetus to work toward a future that seems newly possible and immediately necessary. These are moments when efforts that might, at other moments, in other communal and familial contexts, look self-sacrificial, ill-advised, or useless, instead look meaningful, well-considered, admirable, true.

Coles says that it's the uncanny, unpredictable flow of history that makes moral leadership possible at some moments. George Eliot shared this view, but recorded the opposite of Coles's civil rights–era successes. Eliot's ardent heroines were born into a "meanness of opportunity"; "with dim lights and tangled circumstance they tried to shape their thought and deed in noble agreement," yet history did not conduce to their purposes.[29]

What, then, do we do in the dim lights, the tangled circumstance? The moments that are unpropitious, perhaps even kind of hopeless? The moments when history offers no tailwind? What do we do right now?

I do not believe in the socially transformative force of great literature. (There are those who do and I am not one of them.) Reading George Eliot will not solve our problems. Even after Oprah, we can name the two or three English novels—out of tens of thousands and three centuries of publication—that made measurable social change: Harriet Beecher Stowe's *Uncle Tom's Cabin*, Upton Sinclair's *The Jungle*, maybe Charles Dickens's *Oliver Twist*. That's not a particularly strong record. Books and texts on their own have limited power. Newspaper clippings do not speak for themselves.[30]

I have spent fifteen years teaching material that demands action in response. Yet I have rarely said to my students, "We have a responsibility to act because of what we know, because of the social capital we have as educated citizens." I have been afraid of stepping beyond my job description. But "English literature" is not a sufficient description of my project; it never has been. I need a license for thinking of myself as a civic educator.

Clearly, it is time to hesitate less. I am not the twenty-five-year-old who designed this course; I am no longer mistakable for my college students. I have brought three children into the world, written two books, taught hundreds of students, and not a few teachers. I must not be afraid to lead, in Coles's sense: to be one of those social forces approving and encouraging certain kinds of choice. God knows there is no shortage of influences pushing young people toward lives of self-aggrandizement without any fear of overstepping. At Beit Rabban, we educated, without indoctrinating. We led, without forcing. I need the confidence to believe this is acceptable work in the American university.[31]

So what to do? I could consider coordinating my courses with the university's service learning program.[32] I could develop a course on moral revolutions: how do societies undergo massive shifts in self-understanding and ideas of the good, so that what one age finds morally tolerable—slavery, for example—becomes unimaginable to its successor? We could do the work of guessing what future generations will find shocking and mind-boggling about the social orders we take for granted.[33] We could think toward action.

In fact, I can imagine syllabi for all sorts of new courses. But the very ease with which I can close my eyes and dream up new plans of study makes me uneasy, as if I am not identifying my problem correctly.

◆ ◆ ◆

Sitting at my desk the next day as the students enter, I watch each one choose a chair, sit down, set down their bag, take out their materials, settle in. And in something like a mirage, I suddenly see absence instead of presence. For each student in his or her seat, finite and inexchangeable for any other human being in the world, I imagine hundreds of students who will never sit in these chairs, never walk a university campus. They are easy to discount because they take up no room.

My invisible students are Americans, too. A meaningful education in the pursuit of life, liberty, and happiness is their right, too. Where are their chairs?

In this moment, I know that while my questions about knowledge and action are good and worthy ones, the teaching problem I am facing is not the syllabus. It's not my relation to the syllabus. It's the student roster. It is not a philosophy of democratic action I am missing in my classroom; it's a better version of the practice. And it's not my students' action I am missing; it's my own.

BEIT RABBAN, JUNE 1993

What will we do with our *tzedaka*? All year, we have considered need and tried to help where we could. Our collection of forty dollars poses new challenges and opportunities for teaching. How does one allocate funds wisely?[34]

We know that the children are thinking of Andy on the corner but we want them to see that we make important decisions like this one collectively and carefully. That means we need a little time. Monday morning, we hang a list on the wall with the question, "Where will we give our *tzedaka*?" We tell the kids they will have until Friday to write down any ideas and to mull the ideas other kids put up.

When Friday comes, the children get the chance to describe their ideas, and together, we discuss the options. They range from medical research ("how to help sick people in hospitals") to "toys for kids who don't have any," to two organizations they know, Jewish Home and Hospital and Project Ore. But when we vote, the favorite plan is "Gv to Pr Pppla." Give to poor people.

Taly and I suggest contributing our funds to an organization that will give it to poor people, so that as many people as possible can be helped and the money will be wisely used. But the class is not interested in our proposal. They are ready, then and there, to take the pennies, dimes, and quarters in our yogurt container, walk down the street, and give it all to Andy. His need is evident.

Yet now having learned all about homes and buildings, having considered on our own and with the man from NY Cares what homes are really for, *homeless* means something new and more specific. If Andy is hungry, how can we best help him? He has no kitchen or utensils, and nowhere to store supplies. If we hand him a container full of coins, we can't help anyone else at the same time and he will have to spend it all on expensive ready-made food.

We come up with a more careful plan. The kids will entrust Taly and me to take the forty dollars and buy peanut butter and jelly, bread, and bananas, enough for lots of meals. Then we can use our classroom, a "home" we are fortunate to have, to prepare the food. When one child suggests that we can leave bags for people at the park, another child responds that the person who finds it may worry that it is not fresh or that it is dangerous, or maybe just lost or left behind. We decide to write notes to put inside the bags to reassure anyone hungry that this food is meant for them. Reading-writing workshop goes to the industry of preparing these notes.

The next morning we come in with supplies and during Hebrew immersion time, we make the sandwiches and pack them in bags. Then we get ready for our foray. We talk about how we will give the sandwiches, what we might say, how important it is not just to give the food and rush off, but to look at the person and offer it to him or her with kindness. We talk through what will happen if someone doesn't want a sandwich, or is angry at us for offering. We talk about how sometimes people on the street haven't had a chance to wash or change clothes for a while. Then we head out to the street.

On the corner of 86th and Columbus, we encounter Andy. He is eager for our bag and greets the child who hands it to him by name, saying, "Hey Ari!" Thanking us, he adds, "I never say no to food," and we wave good-bye. It has been a happy exchange.

But on the next block, we spot a man standing by the window of a restaurant, whispering, "Just some soup."

I don't know how this second effort will go, but I tap Yonatan on the shoulder and he immediately responds, approaching the man with great seriousness, while checking over his shoulder to make sure we are all still behind him.

"Sir? Sir, we have some sandwiches we made. Do you want them?"

The man pauses and puts out his hand for Yonatan's high five. I hold my breath but Yonatan offers a ready response and the man says: "My buddy, that's sure nice of you. You be safe, you and all your friends. Be safe. Be safe."

Yonatan hands him the bag and backs away from him, while the man nods and says, "I am hungry."

We have more bags than we find people on the emptying streets of Giuliani's New York. While some children want to take bags home with them, anticipating the homeless people in their own neighborhoods, we also decide to leave some bags in the park.

The following week in community service we decide that it is worth writing a letter to our leaders and representatives in New York and Washington, DC, seeking their help. This is not a problem we can address sufficiently on our own.

A letter is a project of its own. We will take notes as a class on what ideas we would like to include; group the ideas logically in preparation for drafting; and draft a letter out loud, with the teachers transcribing on large newsprint with marker. Then we will edit on that paper. Finally, a teacher will type the letter and children will address envelopes to the White House, Senate, and House of Representatives. A copy will go home to parents as well. No step will be invisible to the children.

When we had begun studying buildings and homes, the White House had been one of the several images we considered. This was not any one man or woman's home, but a home to outlast its serial inhabitants. It was home to an idea of the democratic conferral of power upon an individual who vowed to serve a nation that was diverse and multitudinous, to protect all of our precious lives, liberties, and pursuits of happiness.

We had considered the Mishkan, too: the Tabernacle in the desert where God's presence dwelled among the Israelites, who had given with generous hearts and who had seen the wise design and art of their craftspeople as they built according to divine instruction and human skill. At the Mishkan, atonement and gratitude were central to the human experience, and the human experience of the divine.

We had considered, too, the terrible absence of any home at all.

We had circled back through our classroom, and taken to our own streets, which led back to our own families' homes. It was all one world. One very real world.

And so we wrote our letter:

June 22, 1993

Dear Representatives,

We are students in kindergarten–second grade in a school called Beit Rabban in New York City. We need your help because our country has a problem that our school is concerned about. We are concerned that there are a lot of poor and homeless and sick people, and we want to help them. We know you are working on this problem and we wanted to share some of our ideas with you.

We think that people need jobs to get money. We need more jobs in New York and we need good training for people looking for jobs. Maybe you could even get volunteers to help with the training. A lot of our parents help by volunteering in different ways.

Some people need to learn English so that they can get jobs. We suggest making classes to teach the language. Maybe other immigrants could teach English if they have learned it already; that way, they could understand the people just learning the language.

Homeless people need houses. Could you hire construction workers to build houses for them? Maybe some jobless people could get jobs helping to build. Maybe if they like the building they built, they could live in it without paying for it, since they did the work of building it.

Can you please encourage doctors to make the payment small or nothing if homeless sick people come to them? Otherwise homeless sick people can't afford it. Maybe medicine should cost less also for poor sick people. They need help buying food and clothing to keep them healthy, too.

We have done some work to help people, too. We have worked on clothing drives and food drives, and toy drives for children. Next year, we might do a shoe drive. Also, this year we collected money each week and then when we had enough, we bought peanut butter and jelly and bread and bananas. We made sandwiches and put them in bags. Then we went to the street. We found lots of people who needed the food and they thanked us very much. They seemed hungry. We even left some bags on benches in the park for people who might be looking for food. We attached notes that said, "Dear Friend. We hope you are well. Enjoy your sandwiches."

So you can see, this is really important to us. We hope you think it is very important too. We hope our ideas can help and that they work.

The Kids of Beit Rabban

MICHIGAN STATE UNIVERSITY, DECEMBER 2011

At the semester's end, before my own children begin their vacation, I return to my notebook. The weather has long since become wintry and the vision from Priya's window is white and gray, the tips of the firs barely visible. Coffee cup and pencil in hand, I begin by reading over my course planning, the thinking I did in the August heat before I had even seen the students' faces for the first time, when it was all theoretical. Then I reread the notes I took over fourteen weeks of teaching.

There is always a great deal to consider at the end of a course. Usually, I am already thinking forward when I do this work: what to remember for next time, what new texts or insights should structure the next iteration of this course, how the pacing needs to shift. I write at the end of the semester when it is all still fresh, but I have a whole picture before me. I am fortunate to teach in a college that takes teaching seriously enough to require such written reports on every course taught. These are reports that are actually read, by the Faculty Affairs Committee as well as the dean.

This time, when I sit down to write, I know I will be less coherent than usual in my report because I am still seeking simply to understand. What happened in my classroom during those difficult class sessions? What was it I witnessed?

I write simple observations, jotting down thoughts as they come to me. Eventually, my observations organize themselves into a number of key points. First, we have encountered disturbing information that is verifiable. It is not a matter of opinion or political leaning. We have seen this in public, in the shared space of the classroom, so that it is no longer a fleeting matter between my computer screen and me, but something my classmate may remember and remind me of, too.

Second, we have seen that such data is readily available. Not only is the information readily available but, in fact, it must be positively ignored to not be seen. (Oh, Dickens! In two lines, he captures this exactly in *A Christmas Carol*, when the gentlemen collecting charity turn to Scrooge, reporting that many poor would rather die than be sent to the workhouse. In a superbly provocative present tense, Scrooge refuses the knowledge he has just been offered: "I don't know that." The men reply simply, "But you might know it."[35])

Third, we have learned the unsettling fact that our lives are visible from above, from a statistical, structural point of view. We may feel as if we exist purely as private individuals with no infrastructure necessary, but we have not made ourselves. Neither have our parents, teachers, coaches, or friends formed us entirely. If the state has kept its promises to us as citizens, we are its beneficiaries. If the state has not kept its promises to us, then we are victims of a wrong. Either way, we live in relation to the state. There is no choosing to see ourselves as "off the map."

Teaching in university requires recognizing that new knowledge can often disturb students. In this case, the powerful unease comes, I think, from implication. All of us who sat together in this classroom have a special relation to this knowledge. Contrary to what David said, this story *is* our story. This story is *our* story.

But how will it matter? Will we consent to "know" these facts, or will we, like Scrooge, insist that we do not know? If we consent to know, what will we be called on to do?

I begin to read up on denial, in particular, what the sociologist Stanley Cohen has called "cultural denial," that is, the sort that is not "wholly private nor officially organized by the state," in which a group "censors itself, learns to keep silent about matters whose open discussion would threaten its self-image."[36] This sort of denial is complex because it is not necessarily an outright denial of facts, and it certainly isn't lying. Instead, it is a denial of the *implications* for feeling and action that might come from the facts we know. Cohen describes it as a matter of the stories we tell ourselves to bridge "the moral and psychic gap between what you know and what you do, between the sense of who you are and how your action (or inaction) looks."[37]

As I read, I realize that these questions have accompanied me at least since high school: What do we do with disturbing knowledge about the world in which we live? These questions have motivated projects of action and study; they have shaped syllabi I have compiled and the direction of my research for years.

Now finally, thanks to these students and this course, they have become the direct object of my own inquiry. I want to study denial, but I am also ready to separate from my students and confront my own denials, within the classroom and outside of it. I am ready to listen critically to the stories I tell myself to explain the gap between my sense of myself and my spheres of action and inaction.

I want to open my hand, but I also want to open my eyes.

2 • CHOOSING TO LEARN, LEARNING TO CHOOSE

"Smith" Middle School

Winter 2012—A new semester has already begun and when I return from class to my office, I check my e-mail. For weeks now, I have been writing back and forth to Lisa. It seems there is never a good time to come visit her classroom at "Smith" Elementary-Middle School and perhaps volunteer on a regular basis to teach writing. Lisa's e-mails are kind and courteous, but testing or pretesting or vacation or prevacation seem to make any visit impossible.

A friend in the field of education has put me in touch with Lisa, whom she sees as a gifted teacher, but reminds me that my request is not simple: "I'll see what I can do, but know that there aren't a lot of teachers out there who really want to invite strangers into their classrooms. Especially strangers who are professors."

Then it turns out that some public schools in this district won't allow a visitor without a police permit. A police permit? For an elementary school?

As our e-mails go back and forth, I do what we do in 2012. I google the school. Virtually nothing comes up. Only two hits open onto sites at all. On "greatschools.com," I get an address and two "grades" for the school: a 1 out of 10 from a former teacher, hoping that the new principal has improved things ("it must be better, could not be worse," is the gist of what she writes), and another 1 out of 10, from a parent who notes the victimization of weak students.

On the city's Public School site, I read the following:

"Smith" offers a traditional curriculum enhanced with modern technology and outreach programs to help students excel in core academic subject areas. Our curriculum is aligned with the Michigan Curriculum Framework, and the subject areas taught are: English/Language Arts, Mathematics, Science, and Social Studies. The Academic progress of the students is assessed by the MEAP [Michigan Educational Assessment Program], Benchmark, Accelerated Reading and Math, Renaissance Learning and DIBLES (*Dynamic Indicators of Basic Early Literacy Skills*). . . . Within our technology-rich environment, the classroom instruction also includes the use of [an] overhead projector, video and DVD players and the computer, and cameras are used to assist with teacher and student presentations and displays. Computers are used to practice, remediate and research information.

Practiced by now from my research during the "Truth Telling" course, I scan the demographic chart: there are 915 students, with over 900 African American students. More than 600 are considered "economically disadvantaged"; all are receiving free breakfast and lunch. There are fewer than five bilingual students. Nearly a fifth of students classified as special education.

I click the link to access standardized test scores. If I am reading correctly, there is not a single group in the school that has achieved "functional independence" in any subject area: under 10 percent in any given grade, in any given subgroup, on any given subject, whether math, science, or language arts. Of the students who stuck it out to graduate eighth grade, 80 percent were moving on to high school without proficiency in any of the major skill areas. These numbers fell significantly below the state average, which was not very high in any case.

I click on the other link, where I find a boilerplate letter from the new principal who is "pleased to present" the annual report and notes that because the school has not met the targeted performance ratings for attendance or testing, it will not be invested in for "school improvement."

My googling did not hasten an actual visit to the school, but finally, late in January, Lisa and I came to agreement on a date. On the morning we had set, I purposely did not check my e-mail. If I was going to come at a bad moment, so be it. But I did not want to defer it any longer.

Smith sat at the end of a long, deserted street, off a main urban thorough-fare that connected the area to two interstate highways. Abandoned houses and blacked-out buildings alternated with small houses carefully kept up and apartment complexes that did not divulge whether or not they were inhabited. There were no pedestrians in the neighborhood and the single moving car I saw as I approached was a police car. What struck me most was the silence. I had never been in such a silent urban space.

Smith itself was enormous, stately, and worn. From the outside, this school of one hundred years could have been a nineteenth-century orphanage or hospital. There were no signs of life outdoors at mid-morning. The silence persisted.

I parked in a vast front parking lot among about ten other cars. At the big blue metal door of the school, three or four adults stood simply waiting. They did not appear to be teachers and they did not have children with them. I stood behind them. It was 9:43 A.M. The door buzzed open and we all entered. One man set his keys on the table to walk through the metal detector. Out of a habitual respect for the rules, I signed in at the visitor book on the table beside the metal detector. No one else did.

As I walked through the detector, a buzzer went off. My keys? Or the clasp on my bag? A uniformed security guard stood near a desk beside the detector but no one asked me any questions. Two other buzzers went off. Again, no questions. I walked down the hall myself. The other adults dispersed and disappeared.

I climbed a huge staircase. The hallways and staircases were empty. All the classroom doors were closed, giving no clue that children learned behind them. Here and there were scattered decorations: I spotted photos of African Americans from Martin Luther King Jr. to President Barack Obama, Michelle Obama, and Oprah. The pictures were randomly taped to a wall. The building was dark. I passed a door labeled "library." Instinctively, I reached for the handle, but it was locked. I peered in the single high window but saw no light or activity. I went up to the third floor.

I began to understand what Lisa had said in her e-mail. I had written, "I will arrive around 9:30. I assume I will head to the office and from there to your classroom."

Lisa had written back: "I'm in Room 301. You can park in front of the building."

When I knocked on the door of Room 301, a white student teacher came to unlock it for me. Lisa, at her desk, smiled and shook my hand. About twenty-five kids were in the room. The period was just coming to its close, so I waited in a chair at her side.

A boy, perhaps a sixth- or seventh-grader, walked up to her desk. He spoke so quietly it was difficult to hear him.

"You going?" she said. "This your last day?"

He nodded.

"Tell your father to *call me*," she said, holding her hand to her ear in a pantomime of telephoning.

When the student seemed to indicate that he could not promise that, she said, "Well listen, here's what you need to do. When you get to your new school, ask to be in every honors course you can. You hear me? Every honors course. Tell them they can call me."

He nodded again. He was wearing a white button-down shirt. He looked sad and serious.

She looked at him again, "All right, get going, I'm gonna have to be sad now cause you're leaving."

She touched his arm with affection. He walked out the door.

Lisa and I shook hands in greeting and she said: "That's what transient means. He's leaving, just like that. He didn't hear a word about it 'til yesterday. Some sort of problem between his parents."

With barely a breath, she went on: "This was my group of strongest students. Now the next group: they're not our deepest thinkers. They'll be working on graphing our standardized test results themselves. So they can see just what we're dealing with."

Two student teachers took my coat and locked it up in the small teachers' closet. I kept my bag. Lisa invited me to follow her since the two student teachers were taking the class.

As we walked out of the classroom into the hallway, she stopped a boy also walking out and said: "Say hello to Dr. Blumberg. Would you believe we have a real-live professor here from Michigan State University?"

The boy's eyes grew wide. He shook my hand. I shook his and said, "I hope we'll see you there someday."

He nodded.

Lisa said, "Maybe if she's still around later, you can chat her up, hear a little about what it's like there, okay?"

"A real live professor."

I wondered if I looked like what he expected, if he had any expectation at all.

Lisa's job was to be in the hallway between classes and keep the citation book. A new project focused on building behavioral standards, the citation book was to monitor students who were in the hallway past the beginning of the next period without a hall pass.

In the hall, Lisa hugged kids and they hugged her: big kids, kids ten or eleven years old who in Priya's school would not consider hugging a teacher at the end of an ordinary class session, gravitated to Lisa and she'd hug them, pat their arm, or joke with them. She told me she'd been teaching in the public schools for fifteen years and that it mattered a lot that she knew some of these kids' aunts or grandmothers, or had taught a cousin or sister or brother.

When the next period begins and the hallways empty and grow silent, we walk together to a second classroom. The teacher unlocks the door from inside. The light is so dim I can barely see. Six square tables sit in a square room that was once beautiful: expansive, high ceilinged and airy, with ornate wooden ceiling moldings. Now, stacks of old textbooks rest on the corner of each table. There are no other books in the room at all. A number of students are sitting at the tables with their heads down.

As we walk in, the teacher is yelling at the students to sit down and repeatedly telling them to stop, though I cannot tell what it is he wants them to stop. The security guard follows us in. When Lisa introduces me to the teacher, the guard is standing there, too, part of the team that keeps order here, and since he appears to be part of the picture, I try to explain myself.

I say to him what I have begun, in the last hour, to think of, intently, "Hopefully some day I'll see some of these kids again."

He smiles. "I doubt it."

"Let's hope," I say.

"Sure," he says, but can't resist adding, "not likely."

Lisa walks to the middle of the dim room and I hear her say, "I'm gonna read this list of kids who've got three or more citations. This is a *warning*, a warning. That means, you can still turn it around. But you get five citations and no one can save you. I can't save you either. Five citations and you're suspended for a week."

She reads out the list of names and the students come forward to get their letters. I can't help but enter into a realm of concerns that is clearly foreign here: shame, embarrassment, a reified identity. In all of the schools I know, children's problems are considered private matters between teacher and student, teacher and parent, or parent and student. The privacy I associate with student performance is absent here.

A moment later and we are moving on to the next space: the gym. Here most of the girls are sitting on the floor along the walls, talking and laughing. The lights are out for unknown reasons and I suddenly notice that I am freezing. It's January in Michigan, but this is something different. I can see the air I'm breathing and when Lisa turns to talk to me, the air of her breath rises up between us as if we were outside.

"There was no heat on in the building yesterday," Lisa tells me. "The gym is still real cold. I think we have fewer kids even than usual today," she says, "because they were so cold yesterday."

The boys are all playing basketball as she gathers them for the same speech that I will come to see as her signature: the "I can't save you" speech, whose message is, as she puts it: "you can still save yo'self."

I chat briefly with the gym teacher who is African American and looks to be in his midthirties. He says he grew up here, that he went to Smith, and after high school got an associate's degree, then a master's at Wayne State, and came back here to invest in the kids. This short story of success and return seems itself miraculous in this dim and frigid gym.

Over the course of the next fifteen minutes, I learn a few more facts from Lisa. First, there are three electives teachers for the nearly one thousand students. Because of this ratio, a student will never get to take more than one elective a year–it's either gym *or* computers, never both. And some students will not get any elective at all. It all depends on the luck of the draw.

Second, from third grade on, students do not go outside at all from 7 A.M. until 2:45 P.M., regardless of the weather, regardless of whether or not they have been assigned a gym class. The neighborhood isn't safe enough, even on the school grounds.

Third, there are three lunch periods, so that means a third of the students do not eat from the time breakfast is over at 7:30 until 12:45. Some students have lunch hours earlier. There is no snack time.

I am visiting in the morning, Lisa notes, but after lunch, things fall apart. Students are all over the building and it never really calms down entirely. Anything teachers want to try to do, she tells me, they do in the morning.

As we turn to leave the gym, I learn that when a teacher is absent, there is almost never a substitute. There is a district-wide phone line for substitutes, but either teachers don't want to be assigned here (this is what Lisa thinks) or there simply aren't enough substitutes since so many teachers call in sick so often. In practice, this means that most students spend at least one period a day in what amounts to babysitting. When the school can't locate a substitute, then a teacher responsible for her own class needs to "cover" for the missing teacher. Frequently, two, or even three, classes of students gather in one full-to-bursting classroom after chaotic passage from space to space. Then none of the students—even those with their rightful teacher—will study.

As Lisa puts it, the policy in those hours is, "You don't bother us, we won't bother you."

In other words, the students can do whatever they want as long as no one gets hurt.

More happens on this first visit, but when Lisa, a serious and ambitious teacher, tells me about the substitute policy, I can barely catch my breath. Yes, the bathrooms are appalling (you have to ask a teacher for toilet paper for number two, a student later tells me, and that's too embarrassing, so either they wait until school is over or they go without), the cold is inhumane, the lighting impossible. The paint is peeling everywhere, there are mysterious puddles to be avoided, the library has been locked for months. There are no real books in the classrooms, the guard patrols the building as if it were a prison, and you can't get in or out of a classroom without a key (what if there were a fire?). All of this is shocking to my system. It will take me days to think of anything else. I will write it all down the moment I get home precisely because I can't believe it and I don't trust my memory to hold what seems unthinkable.

But somehow worse than all the material inequities is the conviction that time doesn't matter here. To be in a place where time is slack is sad; when it involves hundreds of children, it approaches tragic.

My mind flits to my daughter Priya's school, the Hebrew Day School of Ann Arbor. She is in second grade. School begins at 8:15 in the morning and students are asked to be in their classrooms by 8:10. At 8 A.M., the principal stands by the school's door, even on the coldest days of winter, greeting kids and parents individually. Siblings not yet old enough for school get a smile or a high five from the principal, who knows their names, too. Down the hallways decorated with student art, bright blue lockers slam as kids take off jackets, arrange their belongings, and race to their classrooms, where teachers are finishing their preparations for the morning. The air buzzes with purpose, with a sense of the new day beginning. Each day is a mini first day of school, even in winter, when the Michigan sky is often gray and the mornings dark. I have always loved this drama in Priya's school.

The children pray each morning, the younger ones for a short time; the older ones for a longer time. So much of Jewish prayer is constructed around the clock and the calendar, around cycles of time ranging from hours of the day to days of the week to months of the year and even to years within cycles of years. There is morning prayer, afternoon and evening, and a prayer said upon going to sleep and waking. Time is consecrated, differentiated. The intense commitment to Torah study itself orients Jews to time: there is such a thing as *bitul z'man*, that is, the waste of time, and it is sacrilege. If time can always be used for holy purposes, then not using it constructively is destructive.

This orientation to time has entered deep into my bones. It is one of the great gifts and great burdens of the religious education I received. But one does not have to be religious to feel this sense of energy, obligation, and opportunity. Any teacher who feels him- or herself working against the constraints of time—so much to teach and learn, so little time—knows this feeling.

At Smith, the die has been cast against those things. Time lost is no loss, which means, of course, also its inverse: time possessed is no form of wealth.

Why wouldn't a teacher take forty-five minutes she might have with a group of students and use it to read to them aloud or ask them to do some writing (no one would even have to grade it, it could just be time to write), play math games on the blackboard, teach them a song, or look at a globe or map?

When I ask, a student teacher explains the situation this way, "Well, it's supposed to be a science class and the only one free is a math teacher."

This does not clarify matters for me. I am certain there is much I do not understand. I imagine there are factors that may well explain why a teacher would elect not to teach. Maybe there are even union directives. I try not to jump to conclusions. But even as I check myself, I cannot help but mourn the waste of countless hours in a building devoted to educating. This, it strikes me, is precisely what a failing school looks like.

◆ ◆ ◆

As we finish our circuit and return to Lisa's classroom, she turns to me. There will be two periods that day in which some seventh-graders will have no instruction.

"You know, since we're just gonna babysit here, do you think you might be willing to answer questions if they've got any? Don't worry, you don't need to cover all forty-five minutes. Just let's keep them busy for a few minutes if they're interested."

"Of course," I say.

I think madly as the kids amble in, mill around, hang out. What can I do? Where can I start? How can I start so that questions even come up?

Suddenly, I am immensely grateful that I kept reading a book I wasn't sold on, Anne Lamott's *Plan B*.[1] In it, she describes going to teach at a prison because her father taught there. She describes trying to give the inmates some tips on writing and how they greet her politely, listen politely, and how her friend Neshama stands up and tells them a pared-down story— pared-down because so are their lives and their surroundings—and they are rapt.

And so, I think, I must find a story within the next two minutes, a story that will matter, that will get past the differences: my white and their black, my adult and their kid, my relative wealth and their poverty, my education and their lack of it.

When I think of my life in the simplest terms, it is not difficult to identify my most potent childhood desire: to grow up to be a writer. That is what I wanted from as early as I can remember.

Lisa introduces me again as "Dr. Blumberg," a "college professor," and just like that, the responsibility for the class is mine.

Standing there at the front of the room, I take a page from Lisa's book. I tell a story to match all I can figure out about this room where the clock has stopped at 11:15, who knows how long ago. It's the story of collecting books as a kid, of having my own notebook in which I wrote. No one read it because it was not for school or adults, or even friends. It was my own.

"It was an ordinary notebook, but it was different than any other. I kept it in the same place all the time so I could always find it. . . . I didn't necessarily write everyday but I wrote whenever I wanted to. About small things and big things. It didn't matter."

What I do not tell them is that I thought to keep such a notebook because I had other notebooks, from school, that adults *were* reading, checking, and responding to, often on a daily basis. I leave that unmentioned for now and let them assume that we can grow solitarily, independently.

I describe saving up dollars for book orders.

"Every time I got a quarter or a dollar, I'd put it in this drawer. . . ."

I am looking at these kids' faces and they've moved from attention to blankness. When I ask, I find out that no one knows what a book order is. Not a single one of them has ever seen a book order, the delight of my youth: those newsprint order forms with the weight of comics, the check my mother wrote (probably this is how I first learned about bank accounts), the teacher mailing in the class order, then waiting a month or six weeks for the Scholastic Books carton to arrive in the classroom, the teacher unpacking it, sorting the paperbacks, this one for you, these for you, carrying home new books, all mine.

I am perplexed that these kids have never gotten book orders, mainly because it is the cheapest way a kid can get a book in this country, a book that he or she doesn't have to give back, that they can own—certainly cheaper than Walmart or Target. Priya and Shai's book orders from school and preschool offer books from a dollar or two and up. Shouldn't Smith kids be getting these book orders if my kids are? But I drop it into the culture gap and instead describe going to the public library. I wonder how many of these kids have library cards or what a public library in this neighborhood might have to offer. The library in their own school is closed, locked up.

So I skip the possibilities of acquiring books for keeps or even to borrow, and talk about my notebook, and writing and writing. My story jumps to the moment when I began to show things I'd written to a teacher. "I'll never forget her," I say aloud. "Joyce Gerber," I think to myself, "fourth grade, 1979."

"She was a short lady who told us to write every single day. She said there was something new to say all the time. And then she would collect our notebooks and write back to us, a different color ink each day."

Two kids in the back are knocking their desks into each other, grinning, but the rest of the kids, maybe thirty or so, are miraculously quiet.

I jump again, a wider jump: to being a teenager, going to college, and finding what is called a mentor.

I take the marker and write it on the board: "Mentor."

I explain that a mentor is someone who cares about you, who you can learn from. "My mentor's name was Mary," I tell them.

"She was a writer who'd written five or six books and published them. They had her photo on the back."

I tell them how I babysat her two kids and tried to figure out what to do to also get to be a writer.

Then I describe writing my first stories and sending them out to magazines that I liked to read. I ask them if they know what it means to be "rejected." No one nods, no one demurs. On the other hand, no one is acting out either, only the two students in the back who are still jostling each other, but quietly.

"I went to the post office a hundred times, I waited in lines with envelopes full of stories I wrote."

I tell them how people kept sending back my writing, many, many times. Tens of times. No one wanted to publish my stories. Eventually, even my husband told me to give up.

As I am talking, I suddenly see the point of my story. I'm not trying to convince anyone to become a writer or to show them how the business of writing and publishing works. The lesson, apparently, is simpler: not to give up, not to let other people convince you to give up, even out of love or the impulse to protect you.

I tell them my small heroic story about not giving up and about finally getting my book published.

"It took about ten years, but now if you turn on your computer and google my name, you'll find my book."

Quickly, I pull back and ask, "Who knows what it means to google?"

No one knows. All have cell phones, many have smartphones and iPods, but no one knows—or maybe no one feels free to say—what google is. Priya has known since first grade that to find things out, you can "google." The capital of Google is Ann Arbor, forty minutes away.

I abandon the language of google—of twenty-first-century literacy— and say instead, "If you go to the library, you can find my book there, with my name on the cover."

The whole time I tell this story, I am wondering what matters, which details will decide whether this story resonates or falls into the culture gap, the big trash can of unbridgeable differences. I'm not sure whether to end my story here, or with winning an award for the book that no one wanted to publish, or meeting people who have read my book.

Perhaps it doesn't matter where I end my story. Maybe the point is just telling it, just being in the room, making some use, any use, of their time. Maybe the point is their meeting a professor. I don't know. I have been talking for about fifteen minutes, which is pressing my luck in any case. I cut off my story somewhat abruptly, no time to seek a graceful ending. I say that now I am a teacher at a university and I ask them what questions they have.

And, amazingly, they do have questions. Lots of them. The first question a girl in the back asks is what you have to do to be a poet.

I answer, "You write, you keep a notebook and you write and you write. You show your writing to someone you trust who knows more than you. You find magazines with poems you like. And then when you're ready to try to get one of your poems in print, you send it in."

It's ridiculous to try to narrate the process from writing to publication for this seventh-grader, but I don't know whether I'll ever get the chance to tell her the next step when it's time, so I tell her now, as if this is some sort of deathbed transaction. It's like Lisa, holding onto the boy's elbow, telling him to get into as many honors courses as he can, because who knows what will happen next. And what won't.

The questions stream in and they all take the same form: "How do you get to be. . . ."

A veterinarian.

A crime detective.

A video game designer.

A pediatrician.

A psychologist.

An architect.

It feels so urgent to tell these kids how to do these things because they are asking so earnestly and are listening so thoroughly to my answers. I'm not sure I have ever been listened to like this before. You could hear a pin drop in this classroom.

I narrate the path from eighth grade through high school to an undergraduate education. I describe the process of application; I note that you can download applications from the web and find out what it is possible to study and what grades you need. I suggest looking at these sites with someone who can help them understand what is on the screen. I tell them about community colleges, liberal arts colleges, vocational schools, and huge research universities. I describe the way many colleges and universities have what is called a *campus*, with dormitories, cafeterias, sports facilities, and libraries. I use the terms *undergraduate, graduate, professor*, and *degree*. I explain the way that many professions require even more than a college education and that, in graduate school, students train for more particular jobs and careers: that you would need to go to a medical school to become a doctor, to graduate school to become a psychologist, to a vet program if you wanted to be a veterinarian, and so on and so on.

I try to break it down, to make it intelligible.

The questions keep coming.

At some point, Lisa breaks in, as if to reconnect this strange visitation with life at Smith, with life in this depressed city.

"Dr. Blumberg, can you just decide to do this stuff later and just not work 'til then?"

I recall her telling me how difficult it is to keep up attendance numbers.

I am not used to making such bald motivational speeches, but now I respond to Lisa's prompt immediately, keeping in mind what she knows that I do not.

"No, you cannot decide later. You need to decide now, to work now, every day. You need to come to school every day. And when you're here you need to tune in. So, say most of the time you tune in half the time, well, every day, try to tune in a little bit more, and zone out a little bit less."

I don't mean to insult anyone. I want to be realistic, to tell these kids that the attention of their minds matters. I want them to learn that they can watch the minute alterations of consciousness that mark the difference between being "tuned in" and "zoned out." I don't know if this is their language, but I do know that in this setting, it is mine, because it is a language that monitors the mind's workings with care and interest. If they can watch their own minds, they can move forward.

The clock might start to tick.

◆   ◆   ◆

After class, Breiana, the girl whose hand shot up when it was time for questions, hands me her notebook. Simply hands it to me and says, "Would you look at my poems?"

There is none of the politeness or the explanations, or even the embarrassment, that I might see if a child at Priya's school made such a request. There is a sense of command to her request.

As these students move on to their next destination, I open her notebook. I don't know what I expect to find. Breiana says to read all the poems except the last page and Lisa offers her a large Post-it to cover that final page. Then Lisa hands it over to me and says, "Okay, Dr. Blumberg, you heard her. Read it all except the yellow page."

I agree and take back the book. I expect the worst of what I see among my college freshmen trained in subpar schools. But while she has one or two spelling errors, and a few punctuation problems, they are barely noticeable against Breiana's vision and rhythm.

> Dancing under the sun where people love and hate.
> Where people kill and save lives
> People use drugs because they never had a love one to hug
> People are rich and sad because
> There money can't buy happiness while poor learn
> Happiness or don't believe in happiness
> Where people will hate someone
> Just because there different
> Where men treat women like there nothing
> And women carry themselves like there nothing while the little baby grows
> And watch her mother cry and wonder why
> But one day she too will dance under the sun
> So will the little boy in class who teacher don't believe in him
> But the streets do and so will the boy down the block with the whole in his sock
> And so will the girl down the street with nothing to eat
> And so will the lady on the hill that is sick but grandchildren can't seem to see
> Someday everyone will learn what efect one efect all
> And will sing
> Dancing under the sun
> Just as I sang
>
> —Breiana Woodson

I read once, then twice. I'd like to help her see this poem into print if she wants.

I decide that if I can, I will keep coming back to Smith. The best thing would be if I can write with the kids, but I'll see what Lisa thinks.

When I hand back Breiana's notebook to Lisa, I hand it back with a long note.

◆ ◆ ◆

When I return to Smith two weeks later, it turns out it is parent-teacher conference day. Although I know now where I am headed, my approach is much like the first time. I drive through streets dead silent, my car doors locked, and arrive at the parking lot. This time, I know not to get involved signing in or asking for any permission to enter the building. The guard stares past me and I head to the central staircase.

As I approach Lisa's classroom, I hear her voice and so I peer in at the doorway and wave, not wanting to interrupt her meeting with a parent.

But Lisa waves me in.

"I can wait 'til you're done," I say.

"No, come in, it's fine."

I'd forgotten: no privacy here. I sit down at a desk in a far corner of the room, trying to give a little space but nobody really cares.

Lisa is looking at the student now. I hear her say, "I won't hang you out to dry." Meanwhile, the mother glares at her son who looks down at the floor from his perch on Lisa's desk. I gather Lisa's report has disappointed this mother.

Now Lisa turns to the two of them and says, "Get it out, talk it out."

But the mother and son are not talking to each other and Lisa looks at the boy. She turns conversational.

"You got a C; it should have been a B. You know why you got that C? 'Cuz you don't like me. Well, you don't need to be my friend. I don't need you. But you're my student and I care about your academic welfare. You're going to live life with a whole bunch of people you can't stand and who can't stand you, by the way. You gonna walk out of your job?"

Lisa's tone is upbeat, not angry. Full of good sense—quick and businesslike.

"Use us to get what you need."

She looks at him as he lifts his eyes for one second and looks at her.

"Now this conversation is over. You gonna use us, right?"

Lisa doesn't even stop. She just turns to the mom and hugs her hard.

The mom and son walk out the door.

I wonder to myself where Lisa has learned the tools of her trade. She is teaching much more than math.

The room turns quiet and I schmooze with Lisa as she waits to see if anyone else comes. She says she is seeing more parents than usual; she's seen four this morning. The school has experimented with different hours and days for conferences, but no option has yielded significantly better results than any other. The parents that come really care, she says, but she never presumes that parents who don't or can't show up don't care.

As we sit on either side of a child's wooden desk, I ask Lisa what she thinks I can do in this school.

She says: "You know, there's a teacher next door, good woman, but she's never taught middle school. They took her right out of first and second grade in the middle of the fall and now she's supposed to teach language arts and science and math to these seventh-graders. How's she supposed to do that?"

Lisa pauses and I consider what I would do if I had to teach seventh-grade science on no notice.

"Well," says Lisa, "she's struggling. Maybe you could show her a thing or two."

"So I teach in her classroom next week?" I ask.

"Let's go talk to her," says Lisa.

Ms. Ward couldn't be happier at the suggestion that I teach English next Wednesday. I say I'd like to teach some poems and do some writing with the students.

"You want to know where we are in the textbook?"

The students are supposed to be studying short stories, but I know I can't manage teaching a short story without knowing these kids at all or how they read. Short stories are too long and difficult when we have no basis for studying them together. So, again, I suggest a few poems.

"I'll bring them with me."

"So you don't want the textbook?" says Ms. Ward. "We're kinda behind."

I can't help her catch her class up. Really, I'm not sure what I'm doing. I'm offering her one period in which she does not have to fight to teach the students. I'm offering the kids one period in which the textbook ceases to be the limit of what is to be learned. I'm a breath of fresh air, I guess. Honestly, I don't know.

What Ms. Ward is talking about is "coverage," reaching the end of the textbook when you're supposed to. I realize that I have never been obligated to cover material someone else has chosen. When I taught K/1 at Beit Rabban, we organized our units independently and organically, and the immense amount I learned as a teacher about our themes, texts, and the disciplines themselves was reflected back to me in the children's own deep, diverse, and sustained engagements in learning. At the university, I have been fortunate enough to have complete freedom in setting my syllabi and its emphases. I have also been free to speed up or slow down to meet the needs of my students, even when I teach survey or other required courses.

I can understand Ms. Ward's predicament. She knows she needs to cover the material—the principal, the Board of Education, and the state are watching—but on the other hand, it's all so desperate here that coverage can't possibly matter. Everything seems a shot in the dark outside of the rare classrooms like Lisa's where someone is in charge: someone with a plan, a strategy, and deep knowledge of her subject and her learners. Everywhere else, a single poem is as good a bet as anything else.

◆ ◆ ◆

A week later, I show up and head to Lisa's room first, where I find her in between classes.

"Can Breiana come to this class, do you think?" I ask.

"Hmm, lemme see where she might be."

A few minutes later, Lisa returns. "She's out today."

I walk into Ms. Ward's class. Kids are perched on tops of desks and the noise level is amazing. There don't seem to be any kids who aren't yelling or laughing at the top of their voices. A kid I recognize from the day I taught Lisa's class is sitting at a desk by the window. "Hey, you back!"

"Yeah, I'm back."

"You gonna teach us o' somethin'?"

"Yeah, for part of the time."

"Like a change around here."

"What's your name?"

"Deshon. What's yo's again?"

"Ilana. I get called Professor Blumberg at work."

"Okay, Prof. I like the sound of that."

We smile at each other.

I take one look at this wild bunch and know that I am not passing out any sheets. I'm going to need to perform again. Ms. Ward is desperately, but also hopelessly, shouting at the students to quiet down, and her remonstrations aren't getting any results. She locks the classroom door. A kid twice her size bangs on the glass window and she lets him in.

In a tired voice, she says, "We got a guest," and I tell her no introductions necessary.

I recognize some kids from the week before but most are unfamiliar. I'm realizing that the group I met in Lisa's classroom was a random mix of kids who had no teacher that period or who wound up shepherded into the wrong class and just stayed there.

"I was here a few weeks ago in Ms. Jones' class," I say. "I teach at Michigan State and my name is Professor Blumberg. Today I want to read you a poem and hear what you think about it."

It's definitely not silent in the classroom—there are pockets of kids whose desks, haphazardly arranged, are turned away from the front of the classroom, but I have a fighting chance since some kids have quieted down, probably just because something is unusual.

"If your desk isn't facing me, could you please turn it around?"

"In the back," I say, "could you separate your desk from your friend's?"

"He ain't my friend."

"Okay, could you separate it?"

"Can't."

"I'm starting now."

Normally, I would go around and get names, even if I won't be able to remember them all, but I'm worried I will lose them entirely if we take the time for that. Speed seems all-important.

When I was in high school, my teacher had introduced us to "My Papa's Waltz," by Theodore Roethke, and I'd thought then that it was amazing. She had introduced me to Elizabeth Bishop, Gwendolen Brooks, Langston Hughes, Emily Dickinson, Walt Whitman, but it was "My Papa's Waltz" that I'd printed from the Internet and brought with me today.

"I'm going to read you a poem. Really, it's a story by someone. See if you can figure out what the person telling the story is saying. What's the story they're telling?"

And I begin to read.

"The whiskey on your breath
Could make a small boy dizzy;
But I hung on like death;
Such waltzing was not easy.

We romped until the pans
Slid from the kitchen shelf;
My mother's countenance
Could not unfrown itself.

The hand that held my wrist
Was battered on one knuckle;
At every step you missed
My right ear scraped a buckle.

You beat time on my head
With a palm caked hard by dirt,
Then waltzed me off to bed
Still clinging to your shirt."

The room was quiet now. After a second, I said, "Let me read it again. You have to hear it twice, I think."

And I read it again.

Again, quiet when I was done.

"Should we start from the beginning?" I asked. "Who's telling this story?"

"A boy," says someone in the back.

"The poem's called 'My Papa's Waltz,'" I say.

"Yeah, it's a son," says a girl in the front.

"What's he saying?" I ask.

"His ole man's drunk," says the boy in the back.

"How do you know?" I ask.

"Whiskey," he says.

I reread, "The whiskey on your breath/Could make a small boy dizzy."

"What are they doing?"

"They're dancin' round the kitchen."

"The boy is small."

"His pa spinnin' him."

I read again, "I hung on like death/Such waltzing was not easy."

"Cuz his pa drunk, so the boy got to hold on really tight."

"How does he feel?" I ask.

"Scared."

"What makes you say that?"

"Holding on like death. Like he goin' to die if his dad drop him or if he let go."

"He not scared. He be happy," Deshon offers from the seat by the window.

"Why do you think that?" I ask.

"He holdin' his dad real tight cuz he love him so much."

I read again, "We romped until the pans/Slid from the kitchen shelf."

"Yeah," calls out a girl, "they rompin', so they havin' a good time. It's so fun the pans flyin' 'round."

"Tha's no good. The pans is flyin' cuz he so wild and drunk."

"Wait—is there anyone else in the room?" I ask.

No one is sure.

I read again, "My mother's countenance/Could not unfrown itself."

A countenance is a face, I say.

"'My mother's face could not unfrown itself': what does that mean?"

"It mean she can't stop frowny."

"She so mad. She mad the pans on the floor. She mad her man so drunk and waste all their money."

A boy who hasn't spoken yet says, "There no way for her to smile 'bout this."

"Hey," I ask, "do you think the boy notices that when he's waltzing with his dad?"

"How could he even see that if he spinnin'? Whas a waltzin'?"

"A waltz is a kind of dance, like a dignified formal dance. I wonder if later when he's grown and he writes this poem, then maybe he thinks about what his mom was looking like. Or maybe he really did see her frowning when this was happening."

"Cuz her life hard," yells out a kid.

"Okay, let's say she's frowning because her life is hard. I'm actually thinking about something from your question: if a waltz is a dignified dance, waltz is a strange word to use to describe this dance."

I read again: "'The hand that held my wrist/Was battered on one knuckle;/

At every step you missed/My right ear scraped a buckle.' What does that mean? What's battered?"

"His hand all bruise from fighting."

"Maybe it's bruised from working," I say.

"'At every step you missed/My right ear scraped a buckle.' What does it mean to miss a step?"

"He trip cuz he drunk."

"So what happens to the boy when he trips?"

"His ear gets scraped by a buckle."

"So it's kind of a rough dance, then. Would you still call it a dance?"

"To the boy it's like love."

"That boy, he imagine a dance."

"What time is it?" I ask.

Silence.

I read again: "'You beat time on my head/With a palm caked hard by dirt,/Then waltzed me off to bed/Still clinging to your shirt.'"

Then I read the stanza again.

"'Palm caked hard by dirt,'" I say.

"He paint houses," says a girl.

"Na, that not dirt," says the girl next to her. "Dirt like collectin' garbage or scrapin' something with yo hands."

"He ain't even wash his hands so he jus' got home."

"But the boy goin' to bed."

"How old is this boy?" I ask.

"He six."

"He two."

"No two-year-old know this much stuff."

"He eight."

"Is he fifteen?" I ask.

A chorus of no's.

"So he can't be too old," I say, "because then his dad couldn't lift him up and swing him around. So oldest he can be is . . ."

The consensus is that he is ten.

"Last lines are really important," I say. When a poet writes, he or she's got to know that people remember the last line because it's the last thing you hear. 'Waltzed me off to bed/Still clinging to his shirt.'"

"That boy, he love his papa."

I say, "You mean because he's clinging to his shirt."

Deshon says: "Fo sure. You don't cling to no one you don' love."

The girl in the front who said the mom was mad because the pans are on the floor says: "No way. He cling cuz he not stupid. Want to get in his bed an' go to sleep before there be a fight."

"Theodore Roethke was born in Michigan," I say.

I turn to write his name on the board.

"He's the guy who wrote this poem. A pretty long time ago. About sixty years ago. I thought maybe we could write a little, too, today. What's the strangest word in this poem?"

The girl in front immediately says, "unfrown," while a boy next to her who hasn't talked yet says, "waltz."

I say, "Write something with the word 'unfrown,' or 'waltz.'" If you want to write something different, you can do that."

I feel immediately that this is not a good assignment, but somehow the idea of asking for more or different doesn't seem possible. The subject of this poem is too intense. All right, I think, let's just get some words down.

"Paper?" I say. "Take out some paper."

"Ain't got none."

Oh man, I had not planned for this. I take a notebook out of my bag, tear out some loose sheets, hand them to kids who appear to have no paper. Suddenly, kids are up, wandering around the classroom. In a flash, the atmosphere has turned jovial.

Ms. Ward, who has been silent, starts to yell, "You sit down in that seat."

It looks to me like four or five kids are writing, out of the twenty-five or so in the room. I try to walk between tables and ask kids if they can think of something to write about with "unfrown": the kids who have been attentive and involved are checked out now. They can't think of anything.

But in spite of the weak assignment and the tendency of most kids not to write, three kids volunteer to read aloud the sentences they have written. While the other kids mainly laugh out loud in response, I thank the volunteers seriously and tell the kids that if they would like me to read what they have written, they can hand it in and I will return it the following week. About six or seven kids do so; otherwise, sheets are thrown on the floor or just left on desks.

The buzzer buzzes and mayhem breaks out.

Without commenting at all on the session I have just taught, Ms. Ward says, "You wanna do the next group?"

I had been planning to teach one class, but Ms. Ward looks hard at me and says she thought I was teaching both. I agree to teach the second group, but I am tired from giving everything to the first group without holding any energy in reserve. Pacing is a part of teaching I rarely think about, but it's critical. I can easily teach two classes when I know that's the plan. But now being asked to teach the second group feels like I'm a half-marathon runner being asked at the finish line to keep going.

Unsurprisingly, the second group goes much less well than the first. I can't get that critical mass of students interested in piecing together what this poem is about, and on top of that, I'm distracted by a nagging sense of discomfort left over from the first class. I didn't tie anything together for them. What actually happened, anyway? We read a poem and we made sense of it, and most of them did not write, but a few did. And then they left. It had been incoherent, and that had not seemed to bother them one bit. They expected school to be arbitrary.

I walk up and down the aisles of the classroom gathering up the loose pages, the crumpled papers, knowing that I don't want to be a part of an arbitrary or random education. I want there to be a rationale—for the students, for me—and talking about one poem out of nowhere does not constitute nor imply a rationale.

Before leaving the building, I stop to talk with Lisa and make a plan for the next time. A clearer plan.

"I think Ms. Ward may want me to teach her class," I say. "Like, really teach it. Instead of her."

"What!" says Lisa.

"She asked if I could come back next week and do it again."

"Oh no," says Lisa, "that wasn't the plan. You're not here to do her job."

Lisa and I come up with a plan that may help Ms. Ward manage, but if it does, that will simply be a bonus. Our plan is to make possible some real work in writing. If I take a group of Ms. Ward's kids each time, her class becomes smaller. At the same time, I can focus on a group and get to know them.

"If you're lucky," says Lisa, "Don't forget, we don't have the most regular attendance record in the world here."

Lisa says she'll look through Ms. Ward's roster of students and some roster she has in her own mind of the kids she encounters daily in the hallways. She'll think of which kids might benefit from some smaller group work; which kids are really serious and could be leaders in such a group; and which kids are just nice kids who could use a break.

I say I'll come back next week and Lisa promises she'll have the list ready.

"Can Breiana be on it?" I ask.

"I'll try to work it out," promises Lisa.

◆ ◆ ◆

My next visit at Smith is late in March and the building is consumed by chaos. An insurance representative is visiting the school and so for the first twenty minutes I am in the building, the loudspeaker blares repeatedly and nearly incomprehensibly: "Teachers, the MetLife representative is in the office, the MetLife rep is in the office."

This loudspeaker is louder than any I have ever heard.

As students fill the hallways between classes, I find Lisa and she tells me she has put together a list of students. Deshon is on that list, and Breiana, but Breiana is absent today. I am unreasonably disappointed. I scan the rest of the names: Tiara, Tavion, Robert Wilson, Unique, Jesse, Antonio, and Maurice. Tiara is talented, Lisa reports, as is Deshon. Maurice has a learning disability and needs some extra attention.

I walk into Ms. Ward's classroom with Lisa and she calls over the hubbub to the students on the list.

"Hey! I wanna go," yells a kid not on her list.

"How come they goin'?"

I try to say hello to a few students who recognize me, but once they see that I will not be working with all of them, no one is interested in friendliness.

"Where we goin'?" everyone wants to know.

I say, "Let's try the library."

"We're not allowed in there."

"Well, if you're with a teacher, I think it's okay."

Before we enter the library, Lisa gives them her signature speech: "This is an opportunity. Use it."

We enter the library and Lisa walks out.

The library is an astounding space. A vast rectangular room at the center of the building, its ceiling soars to unexpected heights and its rectangular windows, at least ten feet tall, let in dusty yellow light along the span of an entire wall. Silent and uninhabited, this library feels oddly like a cathedral at mid-morning. At the very middle of the room and around its sides stand tens of towers of stacked cartons. A teacher tells me that a megastore donated ten thousand books to this school in need, but not the means or the personnel to make the books accessible to kids or teachers. Later, I will meet an older woman from the neighborhood who comes in to volunteer when she can (one woman, ten thousand books?), but she tells me that she doesn't come too often because she needs her adult son to arrive with her and he is rarely available. The boxes are simply too heavy for her to lift herself. Even my own book-loving instincts are intimidated by the scale of labor the cartons represent.

But for now, the library is a respite. It seems beyond the reach of the security guard, the grating loudspeaker, and Ms. Ward's raucous other kids. Here, the light seems gentle rather than poor.

Without turning on the fluorescent light, I guide the students around the towers of cartons to a corner with two circular tables. Of course, kids choose the desks scattered randomly alongside the tables. They stretch out their legs, deny any semblance that we are a group. They are going to make me work.

"Can everyone please sit at a table?" I ask calmly.

Antonio moves from a desk to the table and sits down so close to Robert Wilson he's practically on top of him. I can't tell whether he's trying to bother him or just doesn't know how to sit at a table in school since most of the rooms have only individual desks.

Eventually, we get organized. I say that just like when we were in Ms. Ward's classroom, I'd like to introduce them to some poems, that it's good to encounter new ways to use words, new ways to say how we feel and what we think, what the world looks like to us.

I say all this because no matter where or whom I teach, I always want to establish that writing has a purpose. That it's not a matter of fulfilling an arbitrary assignment or pleasing the teacher, but that it can be one's own thing. It has that potential in the real world.

"Anybody here like to write?" I ask.

It turns out that Deshon raps and sometimes he writes down what he comes up with.

No one else writes.

I tell them I write every day.

I came with "The Road Not Taken," by Robert Frost. Here was my theory: first, I wanted poems that told stories. Second, I wanted poems short enough to work with in one session, that the students might be able to memorize, at least in part. Third, I wanted poems that might, in some way, speak to the students' experience or give them an opening for their own writing.

I had decided that at least for now I would hold the students' attention by reading the poems aloud rather than handing out copies. I didn't want props that might easily become distractions. I wanted the attention directed my way. I imagined moving to written copies in a few weeks.

Focus, coherence, clarity: I wasn't just visiting anymore. I was on task now, ready for this job.

My thought about this particular poem was that it was all about small choices with big consequences, which seemed to me to characterize adolescence. Being a teenager (these kids were twelve through fourteen) was about making one's own decisions, considering options, and trying to choose well.

I think I'd come to this poem, too, as a result of knowing Lisa the little I did. She seemed to stress responsibility, to see it as something worth teaching.

So I read the first stanza of that famous poem aloud.

"Two roads diverged in a yellow wood,
And sorry I could not travel both
And be one traveler, long I stood
And looked down one as far as I could
To where it bent in the undergrowth."

As I pause, Robert Wilson says, "*Diverged*, it's like split up in two."

"Right," I say. "'And sorry I could not travel both.' So there's a man stand-ing at a point where two paths split and he's sorry he can't travel both at the same time. And he's looking down one path as far as he can. How's he feeling?"

"Can't do two things at one time," one student replied.

"Right, but he doesn't know what will happen if he chooses one and not the other. He might miss out on something, right? But he can't do both."

"Then took the other, as just as fair,
And having perhaps the better claim,
Because it was grassy and wanted wear;
Though as for that the passing there
Had worn them really about the same,"

"So he was looking down one path as far as he can, 'Then took the other,'" I offer.

"Why he do that?"

"I don't know. He gives us one small reason."

I reread the stanza.

"The other's just as fair," I say, "meaning just as nice, but it was grassy—so what does that tell us?"

"Not a lotta people travel it."

"Exactly. So the man thinks maybe it deserves another person to give it a try, but then when he looks a little harder, he realizes that both paths are worn about the same. And it's really just up to him to decide."

"Can you picture this guy at the crossroads?" I ask.

Some heads nod.

"And both that morning equally lay
In leaves no step had trodden black.
Oh, I kept the first for another day!
Yet knowing how way leads on to way
I doubted if I should ever come back."

Robert says: "He think if he take one, he gone try the other a different time. 'I kept it for another day.'"

"Yes," I said, "'Yet knowing how way leads on to way/I doubted if I should ever come back.' What's that mean—'knowing how way leads on to way'?"

"You go one way, hard to go back, you jes move on."

While I am teaching, my excitement is growing. In the part of my mind that is watching this lesson unfold, I realize that Robert got that entire stanza's meaning on its first reading. On its first *hearing*.

Timing is so much in teaching—when to draw things out, when to pause, when to move on, how not to lose the tension in the air, but how to avoid rushing and losing some students. I decide to go for the final stanza without any preliminary discussion. I look at this group of kids and recite:

"I shall be telling this with a sigh
Somewhere ages and ages hence:
Two roads diverged in a wood, and I—
I took the one less traveled by
And that has made all the difference."

"Hey—you know this whole thing by heart!" Deshon bursts out.
I smile.
Deshon is looking at me.

"Yeah, I read it first when I was in fourth grade and I've read it many, many times since then. I probably do know it by heart. You could, too, if you want."

"The poem ends here," I say.

"It end the way it begin," Deshon offers.

"It does. What do you think about that?"

Robert Wilson's with me; he's with me all the way: "It be a sad poem, he sad he took that road."

"Why do you think that?" I ask.

"Because he tellin' it with a sigh. You sigh fo' sad stories."

"No," says Deshon, "Sigh ain't sad stories, it's what you no gonna get to do."

This is beautiful, I think. Two beautiful ways to describe this poem's ending. I tell them so: "Those are two perfect ways to understand the phrase."

I go on: "But does he know the path he chose was a sad path? Does he know what he wishes he'd done?"

"Wait a minute—he gone down that path yet?"

I smile.

"No, I don't think so. The amazing thing about this poem is he's telling it standing there at that diverging pair of roads, just setting out on that first path. But maybe while he's even walking those first steps, he's *imagining* how he'll feel someday when he looks back and tells this story, "I shall be telling this with a sigh"—you know what 'shall' means?"

"Yeah—later."

"I'm going to read this whole poem again for you. Just listen carefully now that you know what to expect."

I read the entire poem again, my voice the only sound, their bodies listening.

When I finish, it is silent for a moment.

"Read it again," says Deshon.

I read it again.

"What are the most important words in this poem, do you think?" I ask.

"The title most important," says Unique when I turn directly toward her.

No girls have yet spoken and I don't want to let that go. But she doesn't have a reason for her answer when I question further.

Deshon says, "'Difference,' the most important word, because it like 'diverged.' The poem begin and end with it, so it real important."

I say: "When you think about this whole poem, what do you think of in your own lives? Can you think of a choice you have ever made—or need to make in the future—that you think will be really important, will set you on a specific path?"

Silence.

"Can you all take out a pen or pencil for some writing?" I ask.

I look around at these kids. Not a single one of them has a pen or any paper or books. They've come in entirely empty handed. I scrounge in my bag and find pencil stubs, a pen or two. I look around the library, locate one stray pen. I give kids scrap paper from old papers in my bag.

I say: "Just write a sentence, one or two, about a choice. A choice that seems important to you. Spread out a bit. We've got room here. Take five or so minutes."

I add that I will be writing, too: whenever I ask them to write, I will also write. From the time I began to teach kindergarten writers, I have believed this to be critical. I do it in my college classroom, too, as a rule. The sight of a teacher writing can often mean more to students than any help a teacher can give circulating among them.

At my table, no one is writing but me. I didn't think it would be easy. Writing is always harder than talking; I see this among college students all the time. And so I attribute the current inaction to the difficulty of writing. My mistake.

"Don't make no choices," says Tiara out loud.

The other students look at her.

"Who makes them then?" I ask.

"No one."

"No one?" I echo.

A second later, Tiara adds, "Oh, my momma. She cool."

It simply hadn't occurred to me. Not all kids get to make choices that matter to them. Not all kids are raised to choose. Not all kids think of adult life, let alone their own young lives, as involving a series of options, possibilities, preferences, and choices.

Although Frost's poem does really apply to them—I truly believe it applies to us all—I've taught it without the roots. Without meaning to, I've taught a rich kid's version of the poem instead of Frost's pared-down, fundamental human story of one man standing before dirt paths in a yellow wild, seeing that there are two.

That the world presents us with choices is the first thing.

I could kick myself: not *which* to choose, but that there *are* choices.

"No one chooses," Tiara has just said.

So I say, "If you can't think of a choice you made, write about a choice you didn't get to make and how it felt."

This isn't an empowerment clinic; it's about getting at truths, however sad or unwelcome. That's a path to power, too. I've never believed only in thinking positive; it comes too close to denying pain.

A moment later, I read aloud what I have just scribbled, a small example and an offering of trust: "A choice I didn't make: When I was ten, my parents moved me across the country. I got to make no choice. I hated it that I had no choices. I hated having a new school, and for a while, I had no friends."

Not much reaction, though I know that one of these kids has just moved here from Los Angeles. I tell them to please write for the next three or four minutes. They write, but without energy; they're dragging pencils across pages, writing because they have to: that much I can see clearly.

I hate watching kids do things they are forced to do. If we had more time, maybe we could hit a stride in which they might write because they want to. But maybe not.

Looking at my watch, I ask if it's okay if I take their papers with me to read. I say I will give them back the following week.

As they hand them in, I scan the top one.

One time when my grandma and I went bowling, I hit the balls but made both of them far apart from each other. I was hoping I could get them both but more than likely I couldn't so I had to choose which one to pick. But it might sound crazy because this is bowling, but it just like picking between your two favorite pies but u had to pick one—you can't pick them both. So me, I picked the one that was on the right. I picked that one because I could write with my right hand. But it could have been nice if I got both of them.

That's the Time I had to Choose!! :)—Unique M.

Later, I will see that other choices involve an Xbox or a PlayStation; playing a game or watching television; what to wear; what to eat. Antonio writes about choosing between a banana and an apple: he made a mistake, he thinks, he should have chosen the apple because the banana was no good.

One student writes about making a choice not to do drugs and not to think suicidal thoughts, while another notes that he doesn't get to choose to come to school because his mama makes him, but today he did get to choose to come to the library and he's glad because it turned out to be a good choice.

As the clock runs toward the end of class, I say: "Let me read that poem one more time out loud before we finish. If you remember any of it, say it with me."

When we finish the poem, lots of voices join in. Robert Wilson stretches back in his chair, extends his legs out long. He surprises me.

"This gonna be every day? 'Cuz I like this. It calm and peaceful here. It relax me."

Deshon laughs—a good laugh.

I stop, too, for a moment to listen. It really is very quiet. Nowhere else in the school is nearly as quiet. It *is* peaceful. It *is* relaxing. The sun continues to filter in through the windows, a gentle glow. All the book boxes are bathed in the light. This old library with its high ceilings and wooden moldings is a refuge that has allowed us to run away for an hour. Maybe we could have just sat here: no need for poetry, no need for pencils. Maybe just the large open space, the light, the quiet would have been enough.

The buzzer goes off, loud and arresting.

I say, "See you next time," but they're already out the door, papers left behind, pens and pencil stubs mine to collect.

3 • "IT'S THE LAND"

"Smith" School and Jerusalem

As spring 2012 unfolds, I go between "Smith," MSU, and life at home. 2012 marks seven years since I joined the faculty of MSU and my sabbatical is nearing. Ori and I want to take our family to Israel for the year. He applies for a postdoctoral fellowship at Hebrew University and I speak to my dean about a full year's leave.

Both Ori and I know Israel very well for people who don't reside there permanently. Ori lived in Israel for eight years in his early adulthood and I was born in Haifa and lived there until I was two. My paternal grandparents made their lives in Israel, as have my aunt, uncle, and my first cousins. In spite of having returned to the United States for college and graduate school, my Israeli passport is full of entry-exit stamps. For years in my twenties, I worked to earn enough money to spend long summers writing in Israel. My Israel was never one of hotels or tour buses. There was always a semblance of ordinary life: a rented apartment, supermarkets, city buses, Hebrew. Throughout my adulthood, I traveled back and forth regularly. Priya made her first trip with me at ten months, in order to meet her great-grandmother, and in 2010, we took both Priya and Shai to Israel for ten weeks. In our home in Ann Arbor, we read, speak, pray, and sing in Hebrew. Our lives are stretched taut between these two places and languages.

"My heart is in the east but I am at the very end of the west" (*Libi b'mizrach, va'anokhi b'sof ma'arav*), said Yehudah HaLevi, the twelfth-century Spanish poet.

Each member of our family is a dual citizen.

Five people, ten passports.

And so we begin to prepare. Coordinating the rental of an apartment in Jerusalem and tenants for our own house in Ann Arbor is not easy, but it is nothing compared to researching schools from across the world. While in Ann Arbor, our children attend the sole Jewish day school in town; in Israel, they will go to public schools for the first time in their life. Public school runs in Hebrew, responds to the Jewish calendar, and if you enroll in the system's religious track, provides an education in the traditional texts we want our kids to learn from early on. Likewise, public schools in Israel are filled with observant Jewish children; Ann Arbor's public schools certainly are not.

I call multiple friends in Jerusalem, who themselves introduce me to friends in the know, and over the course of a month or two, I learn a great deal about a number of local schools and kindergartens. I go to their websites; some are better, some worse. I want to know what subjects the schools teach, how they teach them, how many kids are in a class. I want to know if my children will sit in a desk all day being talked at, being tested, being fed information, or if they will they learn through discussion and deep investigation of the texts they encounter, as I prefer. What will the social life be like? What is the playground like? Where do the teachers come from? Where do the families come from? Do the children in the school like to go to school? What languages do they speak? I wonder about gender politics. Do girls learn everything boys learn? What are the implicit messages girls get about their potential? And how does this school approach the biggest political challenges facing Israel: the relations between Arabs and Jews/Palestinians and Israelis, and the future of a democratic state?

I wanted to know all of this before I signed on.

As I engage in this extensive research, talking to people I know and phoning people I don't know at odd hours to make up for the difference between time zones, it strikes me that I am acting out my belief that, after families, schools are the single most important force in the lives of children. That I feel impelled to make super-informed choices reflects my conviction that schools make all the difference in a child's present and future. Of course, when one considers Smith School—a bad school, by any measure, and a school that few parents see themselves as having the freedom to reject or remake—and, on the other hand, Beit Rabban—an outstanding school, chosen by parents who, like me, have the resources and the will to investigate among options—my conviction does not seem exaggerated.

But as my research wears on, I begin to consider the immense space between a failing school and a superb school. Should I begin to think in terms of a "good-enough" school? What about all the kids out there who survive mediocre schooling and go on to be exemplary people who take pleasure and find meaning in the work they choose? What if school is . . . only school?

Looking for advice, I call Devora, of Beit Rabban, who lives in New York but has spent several years living with her family in Israel; some of her grown children now live there. She tells me that when one of her daughters was five, she switched her back and forth between Israeli kindergartens three times, finally ending in the place she had begun, no happier on the second landing.

"How do I choose a school?" I asked her.

She said that in their case, she knew they wouldn't find a school that would be exactly what they wanted. Thinking realistically, she decided that she would narrow it down to the three things that were most important to her and look for a school that had them.

"But pretty soon," she says, "it became clear that we were not going to find that school that would provide the three things we thought were absolutely indispensable. So I decided that if I could find a school that had *one* of those things, we'd be pretty lucky."

One of her sons, she said, had gone to a school that she and her husband had chosen because its environment cultivated a genuine religious sensibility in its students. The school's teachers modeled a way to respond to everyday and extraordinary events in the world as people deeply, vibrantly aware of God's role in human life, attuned to and seeking something beyond the material world. This core came through in their approach to prayer, their teaching of Torah, and their consideration of relations among kids. In this dimension, which was crucial to her, the school supported and supplemented her family's values.

Immediately, I wondered out loud, "What about open-mindedness?"

I knew from experience the ways a religious sensibility could take its sacrifices.

"I would be very glad if the school could model that too," she said.

But she took heart from the fact that she thought open-mindedness was a particularly difficult value to kill.

"It's just hard for me to imagine our kids coming out of our house closed-minded. Maybe because it's a habit of thought. Once it's turned on, it's hard to turn off."

These were not simple questions; that was clear.

Religious sensibility. Open-mindedness. Intellectual curiosity. Aesthetic sensitivity. Drive and diligence. A deep attention to the needs of others.

Some of these things overlapped, some did not. Some we might be able to cultivate successfully at home; others would be more difficult without the surrounding "village." Compromise would be necessary. In the best-case scenario, there would be important consonances between school and home, but there might be conflict and contest, too.

It occurred to me that in the case of my own elementary education, school and home had been united in the most material ways. My parents were among the founders of my first school, the Hebrew Day School of Ann Arbor, securing grants and permits to open it in 1975, ordering its books, interviewing its teachers, my mother baking rugelach and cookies to raise money, and holding late night meetings in our family room. My father and maternal grandfather had literally hammered together the cots we rested on daily in kindergarten and had stood on ladders decorating the walls and bulletin boards in advance of the tiny school's opening. My father had served as the second president of the school, and my mother had taught in its kindergarten.

Later, when my family moved to Chicago in 1980, my mother had taught in my school there, a Solomon Schechter Jewish Day School, as well. My younger sister had made a habit of running away from kindergarten to my mother's Learning Center down the hall when she needed to see her. My early world was thus unusually harmonious, though I did not appreciate the rarity of this, just as most children take the givens of their life for granted.

This sense of school as a safe home carried on to the next generation, as my daughter Priya began kindergarten in the Hebrew Day School of Ann Arbor, thirty years after her grandparents had founded it. Her sense of belonging, her belief that she would be heard in the halls and rooms of the school, and my belief as a parent that I would be heard, flowed naturally from our history. One day, she came home with a book from the school library with a bookplate hanging on from the 1970s, identifying it as a donation from my parents in honor of one of my birthdays. The librarian had given it back to her as a gift.

When I began to teach, Beit Rabban felt familial to me, too. Devora's own children all studied there—she nursed her fourth child in its tiny office in between teaching and meetings—and the school was so small and intimate that to consider it an institution seemed grandiose. All adults went by first names, all the children knew all the grown-ups, and the ties were tight.

Now, in 2012, as I investigate Jewish schools across the world, I contemplate for the first time the idea of sending my children to schools that may be big and impersonal; that may pose problems and conflicts that might be impossible to resolve, but will need simply to be survived; where I will stand outside the school's infrastructure as a witness more than a participant. Maybe my children will go to a school that in some ways—very few, I hope—resembles Smith School.

I want my children to feel safe in school, as I want all children to feel safe in their schools. I want them to learn well, with interest and curiosity, so that everything they learn encourages them to want to learn more. I want them to be treated with respect by teachers and other students. I want them to believe that each child in the classroom is valuable, no matter how he or she learns or looks. I want them to have at least a small corner or moment in the school that is calm and peaceful. If home is hard, I want school to be a respite. I want school to be a place of routine and reason, but also of emotion and passion. I want it to be a good world. Public or private, secular or religious, big or small, I want it to be good.

◆　◆　◆

Pablo Neruda is my next poet at Smith. I bring my slim, silver, bilingual volume of Neruda, and when we settle around the table in the library I am eager to share this new voice with the students of two weeks ago, but only four of the eight faces are familiar. The other four I anticipated are absent from school today and so at the doorway to Ms. Ward's room, other students run to self-assign themselves, trailing the first ones out of the classroom without asking anyone's permission.

Lisa does not stop the students and I don't either, but I have to cut it off somewhere, and so the ninth and tenth kid trying to find their way out Ms. Ward's door don't make it. This feels terrible. I know the stakes are low, and yet leaving eager kids behind is not my business.

Here, in the dim, high-ceilinged, once-elegant library, I begin again.

With four students new to the group, I feel I am starting from the beginning. Lisa has described to me in the abstract the challenge that absences pose to continuous learning. But I feel it myself now. Each time I come back to Smith, I find myself surprised anew by the givens, the way they can set you back and make ordinary things you'd planned nearly impossible to carry out.

Nothing to do but read. Thank goodness for other people's words.

"Pardon me, if when I want
To tell the story of my life
it's the land I talk about.
This is the land.
It grows in your blood
and you grow.
If it dies in your blood
You die out."

It's not the original Spanish, I know, but it still stops my breath. I read it aloud. Once. Twice.

Somehow, when I read this, my thoughts turn to my *bubbi*, my mother's mother. She was born in the early twentieth century in New York City and died there at the very end of the century. Over the course of her life, she moved from the Lower East Side to the Upper East Side, and in less than an hour's time, the number two MTA bus could take her from the site of her old age back to the site of her youth. She had a "land," soil from which she grew, a world in which she was recognizable to others and to herself, I think, too. I can't see her in my mind without seeing the streets of New York.

Today, at Smith, I want to build a concept of "the land." I believe the students can write about this. Neruda is blessedly unspecific: he gives us those remarkable, simple words—his small, dense pile, almost all composed of just one syllable in English: land, blood, grow, die, tell. I feel sure these kids can write back to him.

The land from which each one of us comes, I thought to myself last night, lying on my bed, facing the wrong way, clean bare feet by the soft pillows, book propped beside me. My windows are slightly open because spring is near. At this hour, through the billowing white curtains embroidered gracefully in heavy white thread, curtains which I chose for Ori and myself when we bought this home, I can still see green. It is not yet entirely dark. The green is darker at dusk than it is at day.

In the mornings, when the children are at school and I am home alone on days I don't teach, there is no place I would rather be than propped up on my elbows on this bed, with the sun shining brilliantly, the many greens of our trees and backyard visible through sheer white: peace, peace, peace.

I wouldn't say this is my land, but it is my home. My children safe at school or safe asleep in the room next to ours. It is an intense feeling of well-being. One I know to treasure.

But "the land" is not synonymous with home. The land is something eerier, fuller, more conflictual. It isn't about beauty, just as it isn't about light. The land can be dim and troubled, and sometimes even despised. Still, it is the land. Separate me from it and I am not the same person. Separate it from me and I am diminished in some way.

Even if it is not a good land, it is the story of my life. Even if it is not land at all, but cement and broken glass, weeds that seem to come from nowhere organic, chips of paint, blowing garbage, it is nonetheless the story of my life. We each have a story of our lives: this is our song today.

◆ ◆ ◆

As soon as I say maybe the land isn't necessarily a country, but a place that we grew up in, Deshon gets it: "The land a *home*land, that what it is."

Heads nod.

We talk about the way the poem begins with an addressee: "Pardon me."

There's someone the speaker is talking to, somebody, we deduce, who just might want to argue with the speaker, to say it isn't so. But it *is* so, the speaker insists.

Chelsea, who is new today, says that the one the speaker's talking to doesn't even talk back.

That's right, I say. This poem is the speaker's turn. "Pardon me," and here I go.

"He don't care what nobody think."

"It's his turn," I say. "Maybe there isn't even anyone specific he is talking to, maybe he just feels he needs to speak his piece."

Heads nod again.

We talk some more and recite the poem aloud. Once, then twice.

"I want it to be your turn," I say. "Write about your land. What's your land?"

This time it's quiet. This time I chose well. Ten minutes pass of quiet writing, myself and the students. I gather them back at the two tables. Today, kids are willing to read aloud. And they listen to each other with absolute attention.

One day in 2004 I was about 9 or 10 when my uncle Jeremy got shot and killed on Virginia Park. I still hang on to this because it happened so fast. Before my uncle got shot, he was holding a crazy conversation with me, but it wasn't that crazy. But a year after he died, my granny had died too but just of age. I miss both of them, and they both just died on me so fast it was crazy. But for me to get over that, I had to think positive about it, so it's not that sad to me anymore, but for sure I still love and miss them.

    —Unique M.

E. writes that when he sees people fighting or getting killed, dead bodies, and animals getting abused, it makes him sad. If it were up to him, he says, he would stop it all.

Then C. reads and she begins by saying she thinks her land is really dangerous, like last night, when she wanted to go to the store with her mom and sister, but there were police everywhere and flashing lights. Something was going on two houses down, she says. Her mom said don't worry, but she was really scared. (When C. hands in her paper, I see a little note to me at the bottom of the page: "Thanks for taking your Time to read this").

D. reads. When he was eleven or twelve, he saw a man get shot. The man could have gotten away, but instead he knocked on D's door to tell his mom to get out of the backyard. He died because he was thinking about D's brothers and sisters who were in the backyard. The kids were in the house already by the time the man was on the last stair. A car came from around the corner. The man fell down. He lay in the middle of the street bleeding to death. D's mom put him in the car to take him to the doctor. When they got there, he was dead.

I sit silent, listening.

Our theme has turned to bloodshed. Of the eight seventh- and eighth-graders sitting beside me at these tables, six, I learn, have seen someone shot. Many of them know the person whom they saw shot, whether caught in cross fire or by target. A few mention that they saw these shootings from their own homes. Natural deaths and violent deaths merge, too, in their records of loss.

Neruda's blood had been metaphor to me.

Now I hear it differently. More important, I see it. Red blood, life blood, ER and ambulance blood; spilling, spreading, staining, impossible to staunch fast enough.

I don't know what to say or do next. I am teaching these kids as if something about what we are doing here—studying poetry, learning to write—makes sense in their lives. But nothing about it makes sense. I am amazed that grammar and syntax survive to the extent they do in reports of this kind.

If D. and C. and E. don't get out of here, violence will catch up with them again. If not today, then tomorrow, next week, next month, next year.

I know Lisa knows this and she goes on. She keeps teaching. But each one of these witnesses to a shooting must be living with fear. Twelve-year-old fear, thirteen- and fourteen-year-old fear. It still smells like child fear. Of these boys, only one looks to me like a man. Of the girls, none look like women.

I am sitting with children, in the United States, less than an hour from my home, and there is no way I can protect them. They are already harmed secondhand. They have been assaulted and they will be assaulted again.

The totality of their circumstances is making barriers in my mind. I feel as if I have stopped knowing how to think.

Class time is coming to a close.

I do what I am used to doing. I read Neruda's poem aloud again, twice. A few students say it with me the second time through. I thank the students for reading aloud, for trusting the group, for sharing their difficult experience and their thoughts. I bank on the fact that they can tell I mean what I say. I can't guess what this session has meant to them. At any rate, they have only exposed what each one of them already knew; in their proximity to violence, they live a shared reality. The shock is my province alone.

Some of them hand me their sheets; others leave them on the table. One boy crumples his paper up and shoots a basket.

Their papers are precious to me and I can't explain precisely why. I think it is because they are children and this is the only way I can protect them—by protecting their fragile papers, their precious pencil markings. The papers seem like some extension of their bodies. I walk around, picking up the papers left behind.

I don't know these kids. I am not in their lives, I will not be in their lives. We come into contact for a moment. I am forty-one and they are twelve, thirteen, fourteen. This contact can only be extremely little to them—I know this and I mourn it—but it is something to me. It is changing me. I don't know what the result will be. But I feel harder, less patient, more angry. I know again, anew, that we have obligations to others, especially children.

The land makes demands on us. We owe something. That is the nature of our lives.

◆   ◆   ◆

At home, I read K.'s paper. She writes that it kills her to see the same thing every day. She sees animals that have been hurt or are starving, people selling drugs, people asking for money, abandoned buildings. She says she wishes sometimes that she could help the homeless, feed the animals and the people, get the empty lots together. She says she looks out the window and thinks about her future. What would she do, she asks, if she were to turn out like the people she sees, alone in the world?

"K.," I write at the bottom of her page, "emptiness is hard to see. Abandonment is hard to see. Writing to others can help prevent you from winding up so alone. You can help others—you can't solve things, but you can help."

But in the end, I do not see K. again, and so I never get to give her back her paper. It remains with me.

◆   ◆   ◆

As Passover nears, we reach decisions about where our kids will go to school in Jerusalem. In spite of Devora suggesting I not choose a school unless I see it first with my own eyes, Ori and I choose in the abstract because we don't have the money for an advance trip. My conversation with Devora about the core of the school remains theoretical.

Priya will go to a public religious school in the Jewish Quarter of the Old City. It has a new principal who is replacing a beloved predecessor, but it is still reputed to be among the best religious schools in the city. Equally important, it has small classes of twenty-five kids, rather than the thirty-plus that many other city classrooms contend with. I have found out that the teacher for third grade, Shira, taught the class in second grade as well, and that the kids are generally excited to continue with her. She is organized and serious, and keeps the class under control. I have also discovered that, at least from one parent's point of view, it is a nice group of kids with many English speakers. It tends toward the right wing politically, say friends of ours who sent a child there eight years ago, but so do most religious schools in the city. This is a fair amount of information to have about a school I have never seen with my own eyes.

Shai is enrolled in the public kindergarten closest to our house because kindergartens tend to be bound by district. In Israel, kindergarten is still part of the preschool system rather than serving as the gateway to elementary school, as in the United States. I worry about how this will work for Shai since he is more than ready to begin "school." When I learn that he will have four-year-olds in his class (he will turn six over the course of the year), we debate enrolling him in first grade, but given how little Israeli schools tend to experiential learning once kids begin elementary school, and given that he will be in a foreign country operating in a new language, we decide that kindergarten in Israel makes more sense. We will worry about what he has missed in the United States upon our return, when he needs to begin first grade with his peers.

Tzipora will go to a private preschool down the block from our apartment. We know it well, since our two older kids spent summers enrolled there. And we trust and love Olgy, the school's founder.

We have learned from summers spent abroad that it is never obvious what difficulties will arise, and for which children. We have learned that children are full of even more surprises than usual when you transport them across the world.

◆　◆　◆

Now that school matters are as settled as they can be until we arrive in Israel, I move my attention away from the unpredictable back to the present. I am still teaching full time at Michigan State, with particularly demanding courses this term, and volunteering every other week at Smith. Passover is around the corner. When my dean asks if he can meet with me the week before Passover, I write him a note trying to explain to him what Passover looks like. And what before-Passover looks like.

Most working mothers have the sense that people who are not parents have no idea what has already transpired in their daily lives before the hour of 8 A.M. Before Passover, I feel my double existence as a working mother tripled, as the claims on me as an observant Jew become ever more intense.

I am up 'til all hours nightly, trying to get a handle on the work that needs to be done. In addition to scouring the entire house for any crumbs of *hametz* (unleavened materials), the kitchen must be practically reconstituted. Cleaning the stove, oven, and refrigerator, and covering the countertops is just the first step. Then we must switch all our dishes, both those for dairy and for meat (the ordinary dictates of keeping kosher demand this separation), to Passover dishes. Cartons come up from the basement with Passover versions of all the kitchenware we need, and since the seders and the eight days that follow involve a great deal of hosting and eating, we have a great deal of kitchenware. We switch the dishes and return the ordinary kosher dishes to the basement. And I have not yet even begun to shop for ingredients—all of which need to be kosher for Passover—or to cook for the many guests we will have. Ideally, I would find time for some fresh study of the central text of the seder, the Haggadah, to prepare for the holiday spiritually and intellectually.

Given this list, I decide I need help with the nitty gritty of the kitchen cleaning—the stove, refrigerator, and cabinets—things that someone else can do while I do the more particular tasks connected to the holiday. I write an ad for Craigslist explaining that I need a one-time worker to help me in my kitchen. After considering for a few minutes, I list the pay as approximately twice the minimum wage, fourteen dollars per hour. Within moments of posting the ad, e-mails are flooding in. After eight minutes, I have twenty e-mails; I hurriedly remove the post because I hate the idea of raising people's hopes for nothing.

A retired nurse whose pension "is not going far enough" gets in touch: "I may not be young, but I do know how to work hard," she writes. I read e-mails from an office worker who is looking for extra hours to help support an ailing parent; a teacher needing more income; a number of people whose English is so weak I can barely understand their messages; a laid-off truck driver who says he doesn't have house-cleaning experience but is a fast learner; a home health care aide who tells me no job is too difficult; three factory employees out of work; and people who do not specify their circumstances but promise devotion to the task, promptness, and excellent references.

I am overwhelmed by Michigan, its sea of need that I appear to have tapped into with my simple request for Passover help at double the minimum wage. I skim this list of petitions and feel myself in the unwelcome position of having to refuse all but one applicant. In the end, I respond to the e-mail of a young man who writes that he will work extremely hard. He knows what Passover is, he's managed a cafeteria, and he knows how to get the job done. I phone him and within a moment, we discover that the cafeteria he has managed is at Michigan State. Not only that, but it is the cafeteria in Case Hall, the building in which I work. I ask him if he is a student and he says he is not, but he used to be. He is from Flint and is the first person in his family ever to go to college. His entire family helped put together money to get him started, but the funds have run out, so he is looking for work and hoping to be able to return to college once he has some savings. He has applied to McDonald's in Lansing as a dishwasher, but it is very hard to save any money on minimum wage. I ask him for a reference and he gives me the name of his supervisor at Case Hall. When I google him and his supervisor, the story checks out entirely and I have no anxieties. In fact, I feel happy to have found him and imagine keeping him on if it works out well.

The night before the scheduled day arrives, he e-mails me to confirm. But then that morning, I see a new message telling me that his ride fell through. Apparently, he lives in Lansing. But he promises me that he will find another way to Ann Arbor, approximately fifty miles from Lansing. I get back to my work at home, but after an hour and a half with no word, I text him and he texts back that he has borrowed a friend's bike and is on his way.

A bike?

I write back concerned about whether he can actually bike fifty miles and then do the job I need done. He tells me it will be fine. First of all, he set out at 6 A.M., so he shouldn't be too, too late, and he reassures me that he will have plenty of energy for the work. With the money he makes, he can take the bus back any time before midnight. He says he didn't have money for the bus fare out—about fifteen dollars one way—but not to worry, he's an experienced biker.

I look out the window. It is not a promising day. In fact, the gray sky is lower than it had been minutes earlier, and rain is beginning to fall.

Another fifteen minutes go by; then a half hour passes, and an hour, and it is pouring.

I call my sister and ask, "What do you think about this?"

"It sounds totally crazy," she says. "How's he going to bike fifty miles in pouring rain?"

I call him. He says he has made it to Howell—about halfway—but that there are areas that are very difficult to ride through because of the mud and water, so he is not sure of his ETA. I am growing increasingly anxious. The whole plan seems to weigh on my shoulders. I don't know this kid and he's biking in increasingly bad weather. Time is passing. By the time he arrives, my kids may be home anyway and the job will be an impossibility. Should I tell him to turn back? Is something wrong with a person who takes on such an impractical, possibly dangerous, project?

I google "fifty miles, biking time," and find out that any less than five hours would be a very good time. That estimate presumes no driving rain and good terrain. I also note how many entries concern "how to *prepare* for a fifty-mile ride." Apparently, it's not something you just *do*.

But I go back over our conversation in my mind. He sounded entirely normal, reasonable, personable, logical. His reference checked out when I called. And his rationale for this bike trip clarifies some matters. He doesn't have fifteen dollars available for bus fare and I was promising to pay him at least sixty dollars, probably closer to seventy-five dollars, for one day's work. A bike trip in the rain must have seemed worth it to him.

But now I look outside and the sky is nearly black. It is four and a half hours past the time he said he would come. I call him—texting has outlived its usefulness—and he says he took a wrong turn, but I shouldn't worry, he will make it no matter what.

Now I call Ori. He says: "No way can you let this guy in the house. He sounds unhinged."

I sit at my dining room table, all thought of Passover beside the point. Now I am just consumed by thoughts of Jamie and his bike. I turn on the radio to hear that a tornado watch has just been issued. This is not good news. Just a week or two ago, a tornado touched down in the neighboring town of Chelsea and there was massive damage. I cannot leave this kid on a highway or a back road with a tornado coming. He's already been biking for hours and I don't know how practiced a biker he really is. Whether or not he will ever clean my house, I need to end this story.

I call him back and ask him where he is. He says he thinks he is a few miles from Chelsea, but he is not really sure. I tell him to find any sort of place marker and call me back. I am coming to pick him up.

"Oh, you really don't need to. I'll make it, I promise."

"No, the weather is dangerous. I think we need to put you back on the bus to Lansing. I'll pay the fare."

"You don't need to do that, ma'am."

"I know I don't. Don't worry about it. Just call me when you're somewhere."

Ten minutes later I am in the car with two-year-old Tzipora on our way to Chelsea. As I turn off the highway, I consider how far he actually came. He was close to making it.

But as I head down the main thoroughfare, my thoughts are diverted by what I see before me. I had read about the tornado, but what I see before me is appalling. Trees are literally pulled from the ground, as if by the hand of a giant. Huge trunks, the evidence of decades of growth, lie sprawled across roads and lawns, with roots spiraling into the air. I see a house inside out, its roof upside down. I see furniture piled neatly at the side of the upside-down house. Red and yellow police ribbons block off areas from entry. Branches, some truly massive, and untidy mounds of earth and debris greet me everywhere I turn.

I am on the phone now with Jamie as he guides me toward the rural intersection where he waits. Driving here is the closest I have come to driving in a movie set. This is an apocalyptic vision.

There is no one else on the streets, although the sky is now lighter and it looks as if the storm has passed us by. The day seems to shed hours and Jamie's crazy scheme to arrive by bike seems less impossible and disturbing. As I drive slowly through this maze, I see a bike leaning up against a twisted stop sign. I slow even further and see that it's Jamie behind the bike.

He is sitting on the tall grass at this intersection, with a small backpack and plastic bags attached by rubber band around his shoes. He is a tall, lanky, good-looking kid, dressed in a T-shirt and jeans, a baseball cap. He waves me down.

I lean out the window, "Jamie?"

"Ms. Blumberg, yeah. You found me."

"Hop in."

Jamie gets in. Apologies begin to flow from him, but I stem them, simply saying we can try again another day if he can find time before Passover.

I bring him directly to the bus station in nearby Ann Arbor and hand him a twenty-dollar bill. But in the meantime, I have learned that of the subjects he studied, he is most interested in film. He loved college. He seems like a truly intelligent, curious young man. He is forthright, asking me questions about my work, about literature. He carries himself well.

My heart sinks over the course of this ride as he tells me he will see if he can get the manager at McDonald's to give him an extended shift tomorrow so he can make it back to us two days later. This bright, African American kid, the first generation in his family to begin college, is making about seven dollars per hour there. Who will be the first generation to finish?

While we talk, Tzipora sits alert in her car seat, watching Michigan pass by her window.

At the bus stop, Jamie assures me he will pay me back, and I give him another ten-dollar bill, just in case he needs it to make it back to Ann Arbor a few days later.

And indeed, two days later, he shows up at my doorstep, and does a full day's excellent work. When Shai returns home from preschool, he follows Jamie around the house, up the stairs and down, talking to him and asking questions. They seem poised for friendship. Jamie returns my thirty dollars when I take out my checkbook, but when I pay him, I round upward.

Passover is coming. I am full of questions about slavery and freedom, about roots and transplantations, about generations of souls waiting for revelation and arrival. I am full of questions about the sacred. The trees with their roots in the air haunt me, and one night I dream of Jamie, with the plastic bags around his sneakers, walking through Chelsea with a camera, recording what he sees.

◆ ◆ ◆

As I finalize the plans for our children to attend school in Jerusalem, scanning their birth certificates and passports for the schools to forward to the municipality, I consider how strange it is that my first parental encounter with public school will take place outside the United States.

Since the end of the fall semester, I have found myself following the local education news in Ann Arbor, reading the relevant articles that come across my smartphone, and talking to my friends who have children in the system. I have studied the websites of what would be my district schools, comparing them to other nearby schools. Ori comes downstairs late one night to find me squinting at a poorly broadcast Ann Arbor Board of Education meeting on cable television, eager to see and hear the new superintendent of schools.

I consider what my life as a citizen would look like had I been educated in public schools, and for the first time I wonder how our family's life would differ if my children were public school kids. Until now, public school has meant to me mainly the likelihood of sitting out the Christmas pageant; it has stood for the awkward and difficult moments of being a minority in a Christian country. And it has seemed the occasion for an inevitably impoverished Jewish and Hebraic education.

Public school still holds those associations for me, but I feel a twinge of regret now as well. Public school means, too, being marked as an American by an experience that may differ massively from instance to instance (from Smith, for example, to Ann Arbor's best public schools), but may also, nevertheless, constitute a sort of national inheritance. Does going to public school make Americans feel connected to one another? Should it? Why have I never seriously considered that in sending our children to private school, we have opted out of the fundamental acculturating experience that children undergo as citizens of their nation?

I do not second-guess my children's Jewish education for a moment. I would never give it up. My parents made such an education possible for me, as their own parents sacrificed to give them such an education at midcentury.

To be a Jew is to know Hebrew, to know Torah, to practice *mitzvot* (commandments), to sing and to pray, and little of this can be done without learning. Almost none of it can be done meaningfully without learning.

At the same time, I see that there are, inevitably, consequences that separate us from our neighbors and from the abstract sense of shared fate when local, state, or federal governments pass budgets or make policy, down to the way Ori and I might vote on local millages.

I begin to wonder, "Are we living here but not entirely living here?"

◆　◆　◆

The next time I am at Smith, I nearly get thrown out.

I have grown used to greeting Lisa and then collecting a group of students from Ms. Ward's room, some of whom I recognize, some of whom I don't. Now I always arrive with pencils, pens, paper, a folder to collect material, my poem in hand.

I bring with me papers to return, with my short responses at the bottom of the page, but it seems as if almost always, the student who wrote with me the previous time is absent or somehow hasn't made it with us to the library in the chaos that is Smith. I want to get these papers back to the students: trust is involved, and though my responses are short, they are carefully considered. I think it will mean something to the writers to have been read and to have been considered, but not to have been graded. Yet I don't know what they will do with these papers if they do get them back. They don't seem to have any folders of their own. Do things get kept here at all?

I'm holding my folder and my bag with my laptop, water bottle, sandwich, and MSU student papers for grading between the two groups I've taken to teaching on my visits. I store my cell phone in the outside pocket of the bag. It's between classes right now and the buzzer has just buzzed—a loud, harsh blare—and then the halls erupt with students. As ghostly silent as the halls were, they are now raucous.

A moment later, the assistant principal is striding back and forth in the hall. Holding a megaphone, she bellows through it, "Go to Class, Go to Class."

"If You Are Found in the Hall, You Will Be Suspended. If You Are Found in the Hall, You Will Be Suspended."

I've seen her patrolling in the halls before. A large, imposing woman, she does not seem to harbor any kindness.

She counts down from ten, then yells, "You Will Be in Trouble."

The buzzer buzzes again, and as I gather my group and open the door to the library, she yells, "Against the wall."

I am not sure what is going on, but suddenly about ten kids are corralled.

"Against the wall, hands up."

"NOW."

Students, my students, just about to enter the library to hear more Neruda and possibly William Carlos Williams if we have time, are now standing in a group backed up against the gray wall of lockers. The security guard and the assistant principal have them there with their hands up.

Without a thought, my right hand finds my cell phone. I manage to turn on the camera. The phone is against my body, hidden by my bag, but I can glimpse the red dot: the video is on. I don't know why I'm doing this; I'm simply following some internal dictate telling me this is what I must do.

I'm facing the students, perhaps five feet from them. I need to read their faces to teach me how to understand what is happening. And they do not think what's happening is funny or easy. The public faces of middle school kids in front of their peers are gone. No boisterous laughs, no posturing.

Seeing the fear in their faces, I feel fear, too. And I still have no idea what is really happening here. Are these kids in danger? *Are* they the danger? Am I in danger? Are guns in the picture?

The assistant principal is yelling at the kids, but I can't process what she is saying. I'm unable to turn my focus from the raised hands and the faces, the police lineup in front of me. Ten dark faces, ten pairs of upturned palms.

At the same time, I am hoping my obscured camera is capturing something, anything—even just the sound.

Then just as suddenly as it began, it is over, and the kids are dismissed. Simply sent back to class.

They file into the library and I ask one of them what happened. He shrugs; he doesn't know either. The kids settle back into their bodies as we move toward the tables and sit ourselves down. Their swagger is returning, legs now outstretched, palms again invisible.

I try to follow their lead, to collect myself and begin, when the heavy wooden door to the library swings open. Instantly, the assistant principal is standing in front of me and she is demanding my cell phone. The security guard stands behind her and behind him is Lisa. The security guard gestures to me.

"Who are you anyway?" the assistant principal demands, turning partially to Lisa for an answer.

"I'm a volunteer, I was approved by the principal," I tell her.

Now she is holding my cell phone.

"Find it for me."

I go to video.

She takes back the phone and tries to delete but can't figure out what buttons she needs to press.

"Erase it," she says.

Nauseous, I take the phone back while the kids watch. I press delete and the garbage can icon flickers and disappears.

"Erase it," she says again.

"I did," I say.

"Prove it."

How can I prove absence? And so I scroll through the photos of my kids, the inside of my home, trips to parks and playgrounds. She makes me scroll all the way back to the phone's earliest pictures, my youngest daughter's babyhood. I try to show her there is nothing else there.

I say, "It's not there anymore."

Now *she* takes the phone and scrolls through the photos of my children, searching for what isn't there. I have enough presence of mind to hope she does not delete them all.

"What do you think you were doing? Who do you think you are?"

"I'm sorry, I'm so sorry," I say, my phone in her hands.

"You know it's illegal to take pictures of these kids?"

I promise her I will never do it again. I mean what I say.

She scrolls through the photos again. I show her the video setting, the last video I took. As satisfied as she is going to be, she hands back the phone. The whole thing could not have taken more than sixty, maybe ninety seconds, but I am having trouble breathing.

Because the kids are standing there, watching the entire exchange, I know I just need to teach them and deal with the rest later.

The assistant principal leaves the library, the security guard and Lisa behind her.

I proceed to teach a poem by Neruda about an old man, and the students write about old people they know. It's a good thing I have been teaching a long time because I am still overcome by nausea; my hands are clammy and my head is light.

We finish early and I ask the students to choose books from the thousands of boxed books in the room. They browse and Maurice happily sits himself down with *Come Back, Amelia Bedelia*. He is in seventh grade. I wait out the end of the period; I have never been so relieved when the bell rings. I have no idea what the students have thought of all this, how often they are lined up against the wall, or how often they are privy to a teacher's shaming.

Immediately, I am on my way to Lisa's room.

"Would you like me to leave?" I ask.

I apologize because, of all things, the last thing I meant to do was compromise her or put her at risk. She has gone out of her way to make me a place here, to help organize, to support. "Oh god," I think. "What have I done?"

"Why are you here?" she asks. "Really?"

She is looking at me with suspicion, alienation in her eyes. We have worked well together and liked each other, I think. I had been considering what sort of gift I might bring her as thanks for taking on the wholly uncompensated extra project that is my teaching in this school.

"I'm really here for exactly the reasons I told you. Truly. I got scared. I don't know why I took out my camera. I'd never seen anything like this and I didn't know what to do."

In my heart, I am thinking that while it may not be legal for me to photograph in the school, the "something like this"—lining up middle school kids against the wall, with their hands up, when they turn out to have posed no risks—can't possibly be above board. Imagine it on the six o'clock news. It is not okay that such things go on.

Yet I now appear to be justifying it, as I apologize to Lisa, who deserves my apology.

"You can't photograph here," she says.

"I realize that now," I say. "I wasn't going to do anything with it. I was trying to get some control of the situation. For myself."

Lisa says she is going to need to talk it over with the principal.

"I think you *are* here for the right reasons," she says, but the alienation is still there.

"Please tell him what I've said," I say. "I'm sorry. I'm so sorry."

◆ ◆ ◆

I leave before working with my second group, and as I walk out of the building, I know I may not be back.

On my way home, I call Zarena, my friend, MSU colleague, and carpool buddy, who knows more about my daily life than many, and I tell her what has just happened. When I told her about my first trip to Smith, she couldn't believe it. She wanted to take a Sunday, find a babysitter for her baby twins, and come down with her husband to help sort books.

"Oh my god," she says now, "are you kidding?"

I don't even know what part she's asking about.

"I'm serious," I say.

"They have to let you go back," she says, "you're not the one who did the crazy thing."

"They don't have to do anything," I say. "That place is outside the law, it's not like a place you can reason about. It's possible I'm supposed to have a police permit I don't have. No one even knows when I come or go."

"You've got to keep going," Zarena says, as I burst into tears.

But her certainty is not mine.

The video is really gone. I check and double-check the trash files. I still have old photos of the building from the outside, the heavy door with its graffiti, the high-ceilinged library, with its shafts of dusty sun.

But there is no video of what never should have happened, of what I would have had to decide what to do with, should it have remained on my phone.

I e-mail Lisa the next day to apologize again, to see what comes next. Twenty-four hours later, she lets me know it will be okay for me to return, and I feel enormous relief to be able to finish out the year.

But the uncertainty that has accompanied me throughout is only stronger now. I don't think that six months of working with a revolving-door group of students can make any significant impact on them and they are so used to seeing people come and go that my disappearance would likely not have been noticed. I don't follow an entirely regular schedule in my visits anyway because I have learned that it simply does not matter at all when I show up. There is no order to Smith that resembles order as I know it.[1]

As for my own desires, I do like this work. I like it very, very much. I believe if it were more regular and had a longer duration, it would have effects. I think back to Beit Rabban. I remember the seminars at Teachers College with Lucy Calkins, one of the pioneers of the reading-writing workshop approach. I remember the way she thought such workshops could save kids—could make kids. And I remember the intensity of some of the Beit Rabban children, children with many advantages who wrote and drew daily for more than an hour. I consider the intensity of my MSU students, writing and revising their personal essays.

I would like to keep doing this kind of work, with a sustained group of students, and if I had to leave it now, I would be sorry.

At the same time, I have a full-time job at the university. I have three young children. I live an hour away, and it is not always easy to get myself going on Smith days. If at the very outset, the school had a strange pull of its own, there are days now when all it seems to me is a horribly depressing destination. I feel the impulse to cancel or just not to show up, and it strikes me how difficult it is to maintain one's standards in a place so miserable. When Zarena talked seriously about getting a group of Ann Arborites to come down and sort all the books in a marathon Sunday afternoon, I discouraged her because it seemed a colossal effort for nothing. The school lacks the infrastructure that would make such an effort meaningful.

Meanwhile, a friend in the field of education, an excellent teacher and public servant, tells me that she would never encourage new teachers to come to a school like Smith. While at first I was dismayed to hear her say this, I am beginning to understand what she means. New teachers need encouragement, support, work that will keep them in the system and allow them to devote and redevote themselves to the mission. Working in a place like Smith will beat it out of you, she tells me.

At the same time, there are *one thousand* children in Smith who get only one childhood and adolescence, only one chance at schooling. It cannot be that they will pay the full price for such adult considerations.

In my e-mail to Lisa, I have said, "My aims are restricted to teaching."

But now I ask myself what Lisa has already asked me: "Really? What are my aims? To what are they restricted?"

I should have known since my first visit to Smith that I would need to write about this alternate reality. Without ever deciding to, I've been taking notes on my visits. After the buzzer buzzes and the students disappear with barely an instant of hesitation, as if their bodies are programmed along with the buzzer, I remain in the library, writing down everything that has happened so I can remember it as accurately as possible.

Writing is always a part of my teaching, but usually as a form of inquiry into my own methods. Here, I write because I don't trust my memory for the impossibilities I discover each time I enter the building. I have also taken notes while talking with Lisa and traveling the building with her, seeking to teach myself something, though I don't know what.

I did not plan to write. I came to teach. But now it appears I am also a witness.

In my conversations with Zarena on my way to East Lansing and in my reports to Ori when I return home from Smith, any "ordinariness" I experience on my visits to the school is again challenged. They either can't believe what I am telling them (six out of eight middle schoolers sitting before me have seen a shooting with their own eyes?) or they believe it all too readily because it is what we on the academic, cultural left have thought was going on all along. It is what we insist when politicians on the right or our students argue that we live in a meritocracy.

The difference now is that I have seen it with my own eyes. And this is a difference that cannot be overlooked or underestimated. Having seen it with my own eyes, I need to testify.

I tell Lisa that I came to teach, but that having taught, I will likely also write.

◆ ◆ ◆

That month in the late spring, I e-mail the students from my "Truth Telling" course, inviting them to an office hour during which we can talk further, both about what I have seen in the Michigan public school system and about whether and how their thoughts have evolved. I have always thought it is a sad thing that after a course ends, there is no deferred debriefing.

Three interested students came to meet with me that spring. Two years later, in 2014, I would learn that of my students from that course, one would enter the Teach for America program; a second would begin graduate studies in education; two more would be actively involved in a project to revitalize Detroit without gentrifying it. Another student from a different course (literacy and historical catastrophe) would take a job teaching sixth grade in one of Texas's poorest schools, funding a classroom library through a crowdsourcing campaign.

Had I known the future, I might have felt better that spring of 2012, as I went between my courses at MSU and my volunteering at Smith. But at the time, all I felt was a strong sense of doubt. And so I did what I do when I am at loose ends: I read. My subject: American higher education.

At a Sunday afternoon sale at the Ann Arbor District Library where I loved to browse with my kids, I found a one-dollar copy of a book by Stanley Fish, the scholar of literary theory and Renaissance literature who had returned from senior administrative positions to the basics of the basics: teaching students to decode and to write logical sentences. In *Save the World on Your Own Time*, written in 2008, Fish argued that professors should leave aside any lofty moral, political, spiritual goals and instead rededicate themselves to precisely the job they had been hired to do: teaching the bodies of knowledge and the traditions of inquiry in which they were expert and equipping students with the necessary analytical skills for these pursuits.

The inescapable irony of Fish's stance as a public intellectual didn't detract from his argument, but even so, it wasn't one I could really get behind. The mother in me felt a coldness and an artificiality here. I knew Fish was being strategic: he argued that the more professors attempted to do jobs not their own, the less authority they had over their actual areas of expertise.

Fair enough, but Fish's clear categories—the bodies of knowledge, traditions of inquiry, and analytical skills—all seemed to me far neater in his presentation than they were in reality.

I was well trained to teach "Truth Telling in American Culture"—very well trained. But in this case, I was teaching the literary structure of memoir through a memoir about the Gulf War, and then one about the Israeli–Palestinian conflict. How could I teach skills or traditions of inquiry without inquiring into something?

One of the great and visionary possibilities of the American college classroom was enacted when students engaged in serious study of matters that, outside the classroom, yielded most frequently to simplistic sound bites or rancorous dispute. I didn't need students to tow any particular line on either of these wars—truly, I didn't—and I tended to teach texts that strove to encompass more than one point of view or to give grounds for debate. I looked for the historically responsible and literarily meaningful. I introduced formalist vocabularies in class to give us common ground for analysis—here, I accorded with Fish's proposal—but as long as I taught humanities, I would be entering into matters of human interest. And if I wasn't, well, then why teach at all?

I was far more convinced by Andrew Delbanco, the eminent Columbia University professor of American studies. In his book, *College: What It Was, Is, and Should Be*, he described college as a bridge between adolescence and adulthood where students could be guided toward "reflective citizenship," a citizenship that considered the past in order to shape the future. I agreed with Delbanco's claim that "students still come to college not yet fully formed as social beings, and may still be deterred from sheer self-interest toward a life of enlarged sympathy and civic responsibility."[2]

That was certainly an ethical aim, one I endorsed wholeheartedly. Delbanco went on to describe the particular context of college: one of secular pluralism that sought to educate, not indoctrinate. As I read, I recalled how much friends of mine who had studied with Professor Delbanco at Columbia had esteemed and liked him. Listening to his words, I could imagine this man in the classroom.

From our own moment, I traveled backward in time to the nineteenth century, the century whose cultural history I knew best. What I had been calling ethics, and what nineteenth-century thinkers called "moral philosophy," had traditionally been the foundation for American college education, serving for a time to unify disparate fields from the humanities, the sciences, and the newly emerging social sciences of psychology, sociology, anthropology, and economics.

The nineteenth century! Those brilliant, polymath men loved to try to unify things that were about to split apart for the foreseeable future: the sciences and the humanities, for one; religion and morality, for another—all the big categories of thought and experience. When I got the rare chance to teach my own field of specialization, ethics and economics in nineteenth-century culture, I always noted to students how strong the Victorian impulse was to "unify." Not only did moral philosophers turn the natural sciences to their purposes, as they sought evidence in the universe for a morally progressive order; but because moral law was common to all humans, they interpreted it as a feature and an agent of social harmony and consensus.[3]

For my purposes, what was most interesting was that the college course in moral philosophy had not been just one offering among others. Its teachers and students understood it to encapsulate the social and national mission of their study. Not surprisingly, it was often taught as a kind of keystone course, by particularly beloved and charismatic instructors. Students would later testify that these instructors had made the strongest impact simply by virtue of their personal example. Their task was to train the future leaders of a society unified around shared ideals. The course made perfect sense in a context focused on ethical development.

By the middle of the nineteenth century, however, the culture of university and undergraduate education had begun to shift away from the values of harmony, consensus, and unity to resemble more the university environment we know today. This newer culture supported increasingly specialized study, a professionalized faculty divided up by discipline, and research as the chief mission and measure of excellence. Leaders of the university in this new industrial-managerial age saw themselves as responsible not as much for shaping the character of individual young men but for developing an "elite of experts," to manage a complex and fragmented society.[4] In this new orientation, ethics was reduced to a subsection of other branches of study rather than grounding the whole project of education. For a time, it found its primary home in departments of a newly emerging sociology, and then it moved in most universities to the fields of religion and philosophy, where it typically still resides today.

And that was where I found myself: in a university, in my case a land-grant institution, that retained the aura of those early aspirations to build a nation by educating reflective, morally alert young people, and yet no longer offered them a coherent approach to citizenship.

In my experience, college students at research universities were exposed to all sorts of specialized knowledge and came into contact with world-renowned experts. In the best cases, they learned how to think with more sophistication and how to carry on the investigation that they had begun under the tutelage of fine teachers. College could inspire. I had seen that with my own eyes.

But what did it ask of its students in return? Did it encourage students to reflect on their good fortune at being the recipients of such an education? Did it address the incessant, recurrent problem of life: choice making? Did it set them up to think about how they made their choices? To refine and reconsider what needs to be thought about when one makes a choice? Did it ask students to recognize the moral dimension of life? To consider that life is in and of itself a moral ground, with moral decisions arising all the time?

How was it possible that considerations of this sort had come to be marginal to what we thought of as education? How could we reshape knowledge—in the humanities, at least—as a kind of responsibility, becoming more specific, better honed, and better defined as the knowledge itself improved? How could we connect liberated, disciplined, intense thinking with the lives we chose to lead?

◆ ◆ ◆

Late in April, I make an unusual visit to Smith—unusual because one of my MSU students, Mark, joins me. I had asked Lisa weeks in advance if I could bring him, telling her he was interested in public education, and she had approved. I checked with the dean and he thought that if Mark came independently, the liability concerns would be manageable.

Mark tells me he will be borrowing a friend's car and we agree to meet at the school at 11 A.M.

I had told Mark about the school and its students, but I had not imagined just how out of place he would look in this building. I, too, am out of place, but teachers are always the minority in schools. Mark is a blond, white, nineteen-year-old upstate Michigander. He is clean-cut and always respectably dressed. It came as no surprise to me when I learned that Mark had been a Boy Scout all his life, finishing as an Eagle Scout. In fact, he radiates intelligence, curiosity, and integrity, but I am not sure how those qualities will serve him here.

I gather my students from Ms. Ward's class and Mark trails me. I had forgotten, too, that Mark has seen me only as a professor, not as a teacher of younger students, a keeper of order, and at times, not a very successful one. I am far more human in this setting. Things can go wrong, very wrong, and I am not protected by knowing the rules or by commanding respect from staff, colleagues, or students.

As we walk in the hall toward the library, Mark catches up with me and nearly yells: "You told me it was loud. I didn't know what you meant."

I nod, aware anew that there is no adequate preparation for a first visit.

I introduce Mark briefly, saying that he was my student at MSU, and move quickly to the poem I had chosen for that day. We sit at two tables, listening to the voice of Langston Hughes. I had maintained my practice of working without written copies of the text, finding it more successful simply to read and recite the poetry. It held the attention of the students and perhaps allowed some of them to acquire the poems by heart.

"Hold fast to dreams
For if dreams die
Life is a broken winged bird
That cannot fly.

Hold fast to dreams
For when dreams go
Life is a barren field
Frozen with snow."

They like this poem that I have always felt verged close to cliché. Today it sounds fresher to me. We discuss it only briefly because I have planned for more writing time. I hand out pencils and paper. By now, I know always to bring my own supplies. I mention to Mark that when my students write, I always write, too, and I ask him to write. He takes out his own paper and pen, from the briefcase he had chosen to bring with him that day. I didn't recall ever seeing him with a briefcase before.

The students write more easily than they usually do and most are busy, with pen in hand. Perhaps the simplicity of Hughes's message and his images have brought about this ease. When I get up to go help Tiara, who sits with her head down at the table, Mark takes that as a sign that he, too, should help advise students and I observe him standing over the shoulder of one of the seated students, reading his page.

Quickly, I whisper to Mark that he must *always*, but always, ask permission to read what a student is writing or has written. Also, I teach him that he should not interrupt a student at work. We help only the students who need us in order to work.

As I speak to Mark, I realize that I don't know when I developed these practices—these convictions—or whether anyone taught them to me. Devora? Lucy Calkins at Teachers College? Maybe it was something I read? Wherever I learned them, they have become so natural to me that I forgot that Mark would have no way of knowing them.

At the same moment that I am becoming conscious of how poorly I have prepared Mark for this visit, I am recognizing with sudden clarity the gap that separates the novice teacher from the experienced. Here is Mark, eager, bright, and well-intentioned, without the slightest idea of how to do this thing called teaching.

Teaching seems straightforward enough, and yet how difficult it is: the split-second decisions all classroom interactions require, the beliefs they reflect, the relations they create. Decisions that make some things possible and others impossible. Decisions that do not even seem like decisions: whether one smiles while teaching, or stands or sits, at what volume and pace one speaks.

No, I was not immune to making big mistakes in the classroom (not preparing Mark sufficiently, for one), but what I had was a philosophy. It was the product of years of study, thought, experimentation, conversation, and writing. I had a way to think about making decisions in the classroom and a way to evaluate those decisions.

Mark had sat back down as I'd instructed him. I returned to writing, then glanced around the room. Now three students sat with pencils down. I was used to students of all ages finishing quickly and so over the years I had found ways to help them continue writing, which in many cases was harder than beginning. I asked questions about their work and sometimes that was enough to send them back to the page; most of the time I asked them to think more about the meaning of what they were writing, of what really mattered to them that they wanted to convey. If questions like those weren't enough, I encouraged them to reconsider their beginning or ending point; this could change everything. What about pacing? How much narrative time were they allotting to plot time? They could add sensory detail—life in the body—where useful. They could experiment with different narrating voices and tones. They could give more attention (or any attention at all) to what a reader would struggle to understand or picture in their work.

My aim in teaching writing was twofold, with varying emphases for different students and at different moments. First, I wanted students to see that writing could be an outlet and a source of pleasure, comfort, and relief for themselves, something one could do independently and not only in response to external demands. (This was one of the reasons I never read over their shoulders; the writing needed to belong to them.) Second, and almost inversely, I wanted them to consider writing as a social act, to begin to imagine writing as an act of communication that presupposed a reader who would need to be considered.

My work in the classroom was shaped by these two positive aims. But they were identifiable to me in part because I knew what I wanted to avoid in teaching. Mainly, I hated the idea of students writing strictly to be evaluated, or to be corrected, or even to be approved of. Devora had been the first adult I knew who suggested that praise was not as useful to students as real engagement with their work. Together we had sat at a teachers' meeting and discussed the ideas of Lilian Katz on this subject.[5] Praise so easily became an end in itself; it could empty out an activity of its own pleasures; it could turn effort meaningless and elevate inborn talent in ways that made capable students self-satisfied and struggling students hopeless. It could erase distinctions between projects children had conceived of and labored on over time and the first scribble of the morning. Meanwhile, if adult praise was meant to confer *self*-esteem, where exactly was the child's self? How valuable was the self-esteem of a self who had never learned to evaluate and appreciate his or her own work? It was good for students to respect their teachers and to emulate them, but to depend on them unduly would not end well.

I was both a writer and a teacher, and I wanted writing to be a human activity, imbued with respect, never shadowed by the fear of humiliation or painful exposure, nor shows of power and force. (This was another reason why I always asked permission to read what students were at work writing; risk-taking and discovery cannot coincide with surveillance.) I was not against teaching students to write well. I was not against standards, correct spelling, appropriate paragraph breaks. I knew good writing when I saw it; I knew poor writing when I saw it. I didn't let my students decide what constituted a sentence. For now, I was an expert; they were not.

But there was a context in which I would share my knowledge, and until I had the trust of my students, any guidance I could offer would seem arbitrary and easily abandoned. The trust was simple: I needed to respect them and they needed to believe that I respected them.

I also needed our world to be bigger than school. At Smith School, this was one of the biggest troubles. At Beit Rabban, this had been one of our greatest strengths. At Smith, school seemed completely cut off from the rest of the world. The doors were literally locked and barred against what was outside. I knew this was meant, at least in part, to keep the kids safe from what was outside, but at the same time, the barred door effectively said, "What happens in here has little bearing on what happens out there."

At Smith, as in many schools, kids wrote (when they wrote) because the teacher said to do so. They did math problems (if they did them) because they had to. And often, the teacher was a teacher in a very limited sense. A lot of the time, she was only a failing disciplinarian—a warden of sorts, and a prisoner of sorts.

At Smith, teachers graded, punished, and occasionally rewarded students, but the sky was not visible. Only the man-made ceiling was visible; the aims of writing, math, and all other disciplines were self-contained to workbooks and textbooks. The idea that students would write, as adults do, for real purposes, or because it was an art, was missing. The idea that expertise in math had a life sprouting up in so many forms outside—in architecture, medicine, music, and the web—was also missing. Test scores were the most relevant numbers one saw on the school's walls.

Why learn this stuff? Why learn it from these specific people teaching it? What was *real* and transferable about the life kids and young teenagers were living within these walls?

How I wanted an open door between school and the world, between two places that were both real. The day students had asked about how you become a veterinarian, crime detective, or poet, the doors had been open. A link had been visible between forms of knowledge and ways of living, between childhood and adulthood, between the initial acquisition of skills and their expertise.

I gather the students back around the tables. Mark offers to read his essay, perhaps beginning to intuit that the teacher must be a member of the class in order to be its teacher. He reads a generally dull and clumsy essay about his "identity." It does no compliment to my semester as his professor.

I worry as he reads that the students will laugh at him or begin to misbehave. The essay is full of abstractions such as "guiding ideals," "self-discipline," "sacrifice," and "commitment." To me, it seems hopelessly distant from the library of Smith School.

But I am wrong. The two boys sitting at Mark's table, one wearing a heavy gold chain around his neck, both in baggy jeans hanging low at their waists, nod their heads as he reads. When he is done, they murmur some words of affirmation. They appear to like Mark. They respect him. Some element of his strength and goodness has conveyed itself. His inexperience and foreignness seem temporarily unimportant. I do not understand it myself.

Is it because he is male? Or because he is here, in their school, voluntarily, merging a world outside with this inside world? I recalled an older teacher I had met on my first visit to Smith asking me, "Why you come here to us?" with genuine curiosity, noting that I was the first professor she had ever seen in the school.

As we leave the library, I see the two boys talking a bit with Mark and I remember the guard who had laughed when I said I hoped I would see some of these kids one day at MSU.

"Why not?" I ask now, impatient with the divisions.

"Hold fast to dreams/For if dreams die/Life is a broken-winged bird./ That cannot fly."

The dream that I have is what I would like to be when I get older and that dream is to be a lawyer. Well am only 14 yrs right now my dream might switch up on me 1 day. But right now I really want to be a lawyer, I want to go to a good college and everything now I'm getting good grades but I'll have to keep it that way. But that's basically my dream. I don't want my dream to be like that poem we have read.

—Unique M. (May 9, 2012)

◆　◆　◆

In late May, I am done teaching at MSU for the next twelve months and the year at Smith is also nearly over.

I am newly conscious that Smith School may well be a dangerous place. In googling the school more recently, a television news clip turns up that describes a neighborhood initiative to prevent students from walking to or from Smith alone. The clip reiterated that kids should be escorted by adults, presumably to keep them from getting shot or otherwise assaulted or solicited. That's outside school doors. But inside school doors is also iffy.

One May morning, as I am on my way to Lisa's classroom, I see her turn away from the work she is doing at the table in mid-hallway, monitoring the kids as they move between classes. As I approach, Lisa says to three tall kids wearing backpacks and the hoodies that are not allowed in Smith: "Excuse me boys, I don't believe I recognize you. Introduce yourselves, why don't you."

When the boys give her big smiles and no answers, she says briskly: "Thought I didn't know you. Come right this way."

She walks them down the hall into the principal's office, and when he orders them to leave the building and return to the high school across the way, she walks off, saying, "Nice talking with you boys, good to meet you."

To me, Lisa says, "Thought they looked a little big for here."

I don't know if things feel even more lax than usual because the weather is warming up. My lessons do not go well. The kids can barely bring themselves to keep their heads off the library tables. We cannot sustain a conversation, almost no one writes at all, and I bring the students back to the classroom a few minutes before the period is over, something I have never done before.

Although I have brought in a poem by Maya Angelou and one by Philip Levine, I can't seem to break through the stupor. Even Deshon seems uninterested. Actually, he seems depressed. He is the only one who hands me anything he has written; he has written about betrayal by a girlfriend who has cheated on him. He writes that he can't understand it, but he thinks she is on drugs; he thinks that is why this has all begun to happen. He is as low as I have ever seen him.

Antonio, for whom I have come to have a certain fondness, slinks against the chair and table. Just as we left the classroom for the library, Ms. Ward told me that he has been expelled for "sexual activity," but is still at school.

I don't understand either part of that sentence. Was the sexual activity *at* school? Did it happen just now or has he come to school because someone refuses to accept that he was expelled? Was this sexual activity violent? I have no information and he is my charge for the next forty-five minutes.

The sense of the coming end of year is palpable, but it does not feel good here. There is no charge of excitement in the air, no anticipation of vacation. I wonder what the kids do during the summer hours when they are not in school.

For the first time, though, in Ms. Ward's classroom, I saw some students engaged in group work. When I comment that it looks like the students are really involved in the assignment, she says bleakly, "Yeah, trying to save their grades."

"Okay," I think, "it could be worse." I'm all for the students who want to save their grades.

As I walk out of the room, I hear one girl yell at the boy next to her, "Shut up, I'm trying to learn here."

I calculate that I will be back at Smith twice before the year is done. Late at night, after I have put my children to bed and washed the dishes, I prepare a small booklet for the Smith students that includes all the poems we studied together. We have learned these poems as songs, but I want them to have the poems as print, too.

If only the group had been steady and stable, with the same kids at each meeting, we would have had something here. If we had worked together regularly, maybe we could have polished some pieces of their own writing and put them in a booklet of their own. We could have had a history.

As a volunteer, I have learned that of all the challenges Smith school presents, the most difficult may be the unpredictability of presence and absence. During my first moments in the school, I had witnessed Lisa send a boy off to a new school in the middle of the year, in the middle of the week, in the middle of the day. Since then, I have learned anecdotally that a great many students at Smith have an "old school." Many have more than one old school. No one stays put.

Even within the school, no one stays put. I can't find the same kids in the same classroom at the same time weekly.

When I teach at MSU, I give myself two class sessions to learn my students' names, no matter how many students there are. I have never thought much about this because it has simply seemed necessary to the task at hand. But I see now that it bespeaks my understanding that what matters most is not *what* I am teaching but *who* I am teaching. I can teach lots of subjects within my field—materials are fungible—but the people in the room are not fungible. They need to stay stable. We all need to learn each other. This is the classroom work I believe in. I fail students who do not come to class regularly because what matters to me most is what happens in the classroom.

To be more precise, what matters to me is the conjoint work of reading and talking. Anyone can read a book or poem on their own. Anyone can read SparkNotes on that text and find out its plot, themes, motifs, and so on and so forth. None of that interests me. None of that seems to me like anything resembling the education I am pursuing.

I begin to understand something, putting together this booklet of poems for a group of kids, some of whom were with me for only one poem, some of whom never overlapped with each other, not even once. This project has failed—it does not reflect the real work of teaching as I understand it—because we did not come to know each other. There was no "us." There was no feeling of having traveled a path together over time, liking or perhaps disliking each other, but coming to know each other.

What does it mean to be in a class? It means time logged. It means listening. It means observing. It means you can't think only what you think because you are always being interrupted by other people's ideas, reactions, feelings, questions, misunderstandings, and even memories.

I want my students to remember me, their teacher, but I also want them to remember their fellow students: things they said, how they looked, where they sat.

Not infrequently, I ask my students to begin a class session by writing summaries of the train of discussion from the last class. Who said what? Who responded how? Yes, you can use each other's names. That's the point. At the beginning of the semester, most of them cannot do this for their lives. If they took notes at all during discussion, it is only when I spoke.

I know that in discussion-based courses, students are sometimes confused, sometimes frustrated. They almost always want to know what they are supposed to remember. What *came out* of this discussion? What's going to be on the test???

Fair enough. I can always clarify what ideas and arguments I want them to remember, which seem most insightful or powerful to me and which we can leave by the wayside. And I do that. I sift. I lecture. But the lecture is a *result*. Just like being a professor is a result. Of work. Of inquiry. Of discussion. Contemplation. Struggle. This is the humanities.

My class at MSU taught me—the hard way—not to presume too much. Those students reminded me that any course a teacher teaches is not the same course the students learn. I know there is a gap. We will remember it differently. We feel it in our bodies differently. Time passes differently when you are standing than when you are sitting; when you are speaking than when you are listening. Among other differences, the singular focus required of the teacher is never equaled by the student. I know this more from being a student than from being a teacher.

I will try not to see harmony between myself and my students simply because I want to see harmony. I will not presume that what is left unsaid is understood. Nothing can be presumed in the classroom—no agreement, no shared project.

But that doesn't mean I give up the vision. It doesn't mean I can't still build the space I believe in: a space where reading and speaking train us all in respect and possibly even compassion.

"Shut up, I'm trying to learn."
The opposite of any classroom I want to build.
Speak up, I'm trying to learn.
Better: speak up, *we're* trying to learn.

◆ ◆ ◆

The next time I am at Smith turns out to be my last visit rather than my second-to-last, so it is good that I prepared and brought the booklets early.

I catch Lisa between classes and she tells me that the school district has just fired all its teachers and will rehire many of them, based on interviews and evaluations, before the next school year begins. But placement will be random, so chances are that teachers will find themselves in new schools, with new principals, too.

"They're moving teachers and students like furniture," Lisa says. "If you thought morale was low, it's just gotten a whole lot lower."

As she speaks, I am stunned that more than four hundred teachers could have been fired in my home state and I would have heard nothing on the radio and seen nothing in the news. This recalls to me the essayist Eula Biss's dramatic claim that there is black news and white news in America, and that they sound nothing alike.[6] It appears that black news doesn't much reach whites, either.

"We'll finish out the year, but that's all anyone cares about now—finishing."

I think of what Lisa has told me about the relationships built with kids and families. Not one kid in this school can be sure he or she will see a familiar face among their teachers come September. Likewise, the teachers know the same about their students.

"K–12," Lisa says, "you need relationships for anything to work."

Whatever little there was, now there is less.

◆ ◆ ◆

Flower Day 2012—The last day of Priya's school year comes in early June. Sometime between my childhood and hers, the school inaugurated a tradition of children bringing a flower for each teacher and staff person. Each teacher gets a bucket, and when the kids arrive, the teachers stand beside the door of their classrooms and the children go from door to door offering their flowers.

The halls have never been more colorful and animate. Many kids bring flowers from their gardens; others bring store-bought bouquets from which they separate individual flowers. There are many hugs—you can barely make your way through the hallway—and though it is the kids who give the flowers, lots of parents are part of this scene too. The children rush from room to room, in pairs, alone, with siblings, in groups, and the excitement at the end of the year merges with the excitement of giving pleasure and giving thanks.

The night before Flower Day, Priya made a list of all the teachers and staff she wanted to give to, writing out each name and counting them up: eleven in all. That included former teachers, her homeroom teachers, specialty teachers, the principal, and all the staff.

We have brought some flowers from the store and the precious last of the peonies from our garden, which we did not plant ourselves but inherited when we bought our house. The peonies are both light and very deep pink, and as they rest against Priya's skin as she holds them to her face to breathe in the smell, they remind me how children can flower, too, in the right soil.

◆ ◆ ◆

In late summer, we begin to pack our things for Jerusalem. Priya, now eight, is really reluctant to go—we are ruining her life, she tells us with no shortage of drama—and Shai is not eager, either. He has been waiting for years, it seems, to start at the Hebrew Day School with his sister and now we are deferring it still another year. Only Tzipora seems amenable and that is because she is just two.

I am eager for the time to write and read, and for the opportunity to live and study in Jerusalem, but I am very sad to leave Ann Arbor, even for only a year. Something in me knows that when you leave on this sort of trip, you run the risk—or entertain the promise—that nothing will remain the same. What has been stable and in place is forced out of its mold.

Our older children seem to intuit this as well.

Priya challenges us, "You're saying a year, but can you promise me we will come back?"

We do promise her, because my sabbatical is contingent on returning to my job for at least a year, but we all know that the promise is a legalistic one. We promise her in such a way—"Yes, we will be back for at least a year—" that she knows her worry is real.

I think of friends of ours who are parents of a schoolmate of Priya's. When our friend got tenure, I remember him saying happily, "We're lifers." Ann Arbor was the end of their family's horizon. And I remember Ori saying to me later that he could not even imagine living out his days in Ann Arbor. Not his land.

We are on the cusp of taking our kids to a place both Ori and I attached to young, a place ancient and strong, which sometimes eats its inhabitants but also brings them great blessing. An epic place.

Ann Arbor is a cultivated garden.

Israel is a desert and valleys, plains and sand and rock; it is mountains, salt, springs of water, seas, and caves. Jerusalem is olives, figs, pomegranates, barley, vines, clusters, milk and honey.

Ori will be teaching one course at Hebrew University, a literature survey exploring the question of why people choose evil. When we arrive, I will find a place to study Jewish texts one full day a week. In the late fall,

I will teach six writing workshops for Bar Ilan University. For now, I have no other plans, knowing that I will need to spend a good deal of time helping our kids acclimate. My research will have to fit itself around that aim.

When it comes time for us to leave, the tears all around give me a sense that I am leaving a beloved place, and probably leaving it for good.

POSTSCRIPT

Shadow Schools—Kindergarten to College, America and Israel

August 2015—We have lived in Israel for a full year now since moving here permanently. By the time my sabbatical was over, I had received an offer from the English department of Bar Ilan University. I accepted, deferring for one year to fulfill our commitments in Michigan.

People on both sides of the ocean asked us if the sabbatical year had been a "test year," and Ori and I looked at each other knowingly. If it had been a test, we wouldn't have returned. It was not an easy year, but we had not anticipated that it would be. It was a year of laying groundwork. It was time that made clear what we would be giving up and hinted at what we might realize in exchange. We weighed the solid realities of our life in Michigan against the airy predictions of what might materialize if we were settled—if we settled well, if our children settled well.

In spite of what many of our American friends and colleagues imagined, it was school—not war, language, or the economy—that stood as the greatest stumbling block when I had considered leaving the United States for Israel. (The other obstacle was leaving family.) When I imagined my children's lives in Israel, I began with school, because when I considered childhood anywhere, school seemed to me its central experience. To my surprise, many Israelis I encountered did not seem highly invested in their children's schools.

When I thought about the parents I knew in Ann Arbor, I couldn't think of any who hadn't taken extremely seriously the choice of a school, a district, or a teacher. I wasn't thinking about obsessive parents, but about educated, sensible adults who recognized that school was seven hours a day for more than nine months a year and that given how much time a child spent there and what it was supposed to enable for his or her future, you would want it to be at least pretty good. Some parents were more involved and some less, but I knew very few who were nonchalant about their children's education. When things did not go well for their child, they did everything they could to change or improve the situation.

When I arrived in Israel, many Israelis I spoke to—among them, highly educated professionals and academics—thought their children's public elementary schools were not especially good and they were sorry about this fact, but that was life. (Some thought that high school education was better, but that was still far off for me.) A few were more satisfied, but most parents who had kids in district public schools threw up their hands and said that they had gone to the same schools, that little had changed, and that they had survived and so would their kids.[1]

The Ministry of Education determined curriculum across the country, so teachers, and even principals, had little say about much of what was taught. Perhaps this accounted for the extraordinary number of subjects the children studied: Priya would have fourteen different courses as a third-grader, with subject areas such as language arts, for example, divided mysteriously into four components: "Mottoes and Expressions," "Reading Comprehension," "Language," and "Literature." Each component had a different workbook, notebook, and folder, and there were three teachers who covered these subjects. So much for integrated, let alone interdisciplinary, learning. Most parents were concerned primarily about class size; almost no one I spoke to raised the question of pedagogy.

"They're home by two anyway," said one mother I liked, "you'll see, the day really starts then."

At that moment, the Hebrew she was speaking seemed the least foreign element of our conversation.

◆　◆　◆

The writer André Aciman has beautifully described the way that for some of us, we know a city most fully when we sit in another, distant city—the "shadow" of the first—imagining and remembering the original.[2] The same may be said of schools. As I came to know my children's Israeli schools, I was revisiting in my mind the classrooms and hallways of Beit Rabban, the Hebrew Day School of Ann Arbor, and Smith School. A palimpsest of schools, of children's faces, classrooms, teachers, playgrounds.

I spent the first week of the 2012–2013 school year in Jerusalem sitting at a small desk in the back of Priya's third-grade classroom. Perhaps because I am a teacher, but certainly because I am a mother, I wanted to see her school from the inside to know first, where I was sending her for hours each day, and second, what she would need to know and do to learn and to succeed. To my happy surprise, both her homeroom teacher, Shira, and all the other subject-area teachers gave me ready permission to sit in on their classes, with the exception of a novice music teacher who thought observation would be difficult for her.

In Shira's class, I sat quietly and watched a talented young teacher who knew how to motivate kids and keep order, at the same time that she transmitted a good deal of knowledge. Shira was very likable.

As I watched her, I saw right away that children participated avidly in this classroom but that their participation was comprised of answering questions. They rarely spoke at any length. I remembered the powerful article I had read when teaching at Beit Rabban about the value of making declarative statements as a teacher, rather than posing questions that actually shut down discussion rather than developing it.[3] Research had found that kids tended to talk at much greater length and to allow themselves to reach for more complex thoughts if they were not answering a teacher's questions but responding to her statements. I had practiced what at first seemed absurd ways of speaking to confirm, in fact, that kids *did* have much more to say when I began discussion by stating simply, "I wonder what any of you think about . . ." or "It's interesting that . . . ," and then waiting to see who raised a hand.

I learned also to wait three to five seconds in silence once a student had stopped speaking. Often students resumed speaking after a second or two. Or another student would pick up the first student's thought after having been given the few seconds he or she needed to assimilate it. In Priya's new classroom, by contrast, almost no child picked up on any comment made by any other child and responded to it. Nearly all the communication was confined to short exchanges between the teacher and an individual student. Consequently, it was not necessary for any student actually to listen to any other student. For all the strengths of this classroom, its structure negated the notion that you could learn from exchange and that students could help each other produce or refine ideas by questioning or affirming each other. All the significant information came from the teacher.

I noted, too, that while the students typically answered the teacher's questions correctly, most questions, regardless of subject area, did not have multiple possible answers. In other words, most questions were factual, not interpretive, and even the questions that were interpretive seemed to have a fairly circumscribed set of possible answers. No child posed his or her own question during the days I visited.[4]

What I saw in this classroom, then, was a world in which questions of content—questions asked by the teacher—led to very clear answers that only the teacher affirmed or rejected.[5] These answers always existed already and so the sense of independent or collective discovery was entirely absent. The absence of a hard-earned, rewarding discovery killed most of the tendency to curiosity. Without curiosity and a "genuine act of questioning," what might motivate you to learn?[6] To read on at night, even when the lights were supposed to be out? To experiment? To find answers the world might need? To find the answers *you* might need?

In this world of learning that my daughter was to enter, how would you verify the rightness of an answer without recourse to the teacher? How would you go on without the teacher at all? Also, *why* would you?

I was not persuaded by the idea that third grade was too young for such concerns. I had seen with my own eyes that five- and six-year-olds could learn with each other and share the work of question and research with their teachers. I had also seen with my own eyes how hard it was for college freshmen to figure out how to listen to each other, ask a meaningful question, or search for a possible answer.

Here were the roots of such trouble. Discussion was missing. Learning here meant simply receiving, and the receiving was individual. Each child was being taught to be in it for him- or herself. In this setting, she didn't need her peers; they didn't need her. Lost was the potential of the classroom to teach the lessons of respect for other human beings in the most natural way. No one was teaching the drama and discipline of listening, or the equally critical and challenging act of responding to what one heard. The end here would be the inevitable test of recall and the numerical report card.

It came as little surprise that over the course of the year, Priya wrote very little in Hebrew or English. What she did write was highly regimented: mostly short answers to short questions of fact or reading comprehension; occasionally, a book report; a paragraph here or there summarizing an encyclopedia entry. Editing meant correcting mistakes rather than deepening thought or reconsidering how the piece of writing met the writer's aims or succeeded in communicating to an audience. Developing a voice was no aim at all. Neither was sinking into writing (or reading). Throughout the year, I would be astounded by how much the kids copied from the board.

I could see that the students in Priya's new class seemed to like school and I appreciated this. They seemed happy, and when Shira reined them in, they appeared to experience her discipline as welcome. From what Priya reported, not all teachers were as successful, but on the whole, learning was taking place in this school. The staff was committed, the principal was hard-working, and the parents were responsive.

I could not be enthusiastic about this school, but I was willing to call it "good enough." Or perhaps good enough for now.

It did not escape me that everyone I talked to thought this was an extraordinary school.

◆ ◆ ◆

We did not fare as well with Shai. Another year in preschool was not what the doctor had ordered. From the moment we walked into the kindergarten, my heart sank. The chairs were tiny, and the room felt just like his preschool. Even worse, the yard, which was dramatically smaller than the one he had in the United States, had only plastic baby climbers. Shai was tall, sporty, very well-coordinated, and eager to play team sports. The kindergarten seemed much closer to nursery than to elementary school.

Thirty-five district kids were assigned to his class, with one teacher and an assistant who seemed to confine herself mainly to sweeping and washing the floor and cutting fruit for snack. If a child was bleeding, she might help out, but clearly she was not another educator. Many children wailed daily when saying good-bye to parents, and though there were letters up on the classroom walls, it looked like the year would be mainly playtime.

We were assured by countless other parents that kids needed more time to be kids, an approach I was not averse to, except that Shai, being an American five-and-a-half-year-old, had already benefited from three years of excellent preschool and was ready for real school. I suspected that the reason many parents loved the *ganim*, the kindergartens, was simply because they did not love the schools, and they preferred to see their young children moving about a classroom, playing and talking to each other, rather than sitting stiffly behind small desks in rows, copying from the board.

The best part about Shai's *gan* was that he met some very nice kids, but many mornings were struggles. I could measure his ease in school by the state of his lunch box at 2 P.M. A good day meant he had managed to eat about half of what I had packed; on other days, he wouldn't have touched his food. There were many other days.

In November, war broke out. Priya came home from school asking about the sheikh who had been assassinated. Shai, listening anxiously, asked, "What? What?"—and then missiles began to fall. The missiles came from Gaza and though we were in a fairly safe part of the country, Israel is a very small territory and inevitably, missiles fell in Jerusalem, too. Dull sirens rang through the city for the first time on a Friday night, just as Shabbat began, and we sat huddled together in the basement area of our apartment for twenty minutes. We had heard the thud of a landing but no sirens coming from emergency vehicles, which seemed a relief. Later, we would learn that the missile had fallen in an open field, and thankfully, there had been no injuries. The second siren rang while Shai was with Ori on the way home from *gan* and they returned to the safety of the school. Priya had been just about to board the bus home, and the driver and kids jumped out and lay down in the parking lot with their hands clasped around their heads, as they had been told to do.

War, even at a distance, is terrifying. Danger puts your body on alarm. I recalled a new book I had read in the months after working at Smith, *How Children Succeed*, in which Paul Tough describes the physiological effects of trauma on children's brains and bodies, and how difficult it is to learn not only during situations of intense danger or stress, but after repeated exposure to such conditions. The conditions can go away, but the damage remains.

After the sirens, Shai begins to sleep in our bed at night and Priya asks for a phone like her friends' parents have given them, so she can reach us in an emergency. They both have endless questions about the news. Meanwhile, in accordance with State Department recommendations, friends of ours from Ann Arbor cancel their upcoming, long-awaited trip to Jerusalem.

For my part, I am not terribly afraid for my children's safety. Relative to other children in Israel, to children in Gaza, to children in some parts of

Michigan, and to most of the two billion children around the world, my children are in very safe conditions.

In spite of these facts, it is also true that they are probably less safe than they were in Ann Arbor. And more difficult still, it is true that there are people who seek their harm. For the first time, my family joins the enormous portion of human beings around the globe who feel themselves at risk of violence.[7]

Priya and Shai ask how we could have brought them to a country with bombs, from Ann Arbor, where, yes, you might get hit by a car crossing a street, but no one is trying to blow you up, and when you grow up, you don't have to be in the army. (Well, perhaps *you* don't, but *someone* does.) Yes, a madman might break into your school and shoot you down, and yes, my kids did multiple lockdown drills in Ann Arbor when they hid under tables and in bathrooms with the shades down for more than half an hour. I know that when they are older I can tell them that tragedy does not always discriminate by zip code and one doesn't live life asking others to absorb all the danger and all the sacrifice for you. Still, in spite of these adult truths, I can't offer a fully satisfying answer to myself, any more than to Priya and Shai.

Who takes children to a war zone?

Around the globe, millions of people are involved in the life-and-death struggle to propel their children out of harm's reach. Over the summer in Ann Arbor, Priya met two Iraqi girls in dance camp. I learned that they were refugees who fled Iraq after their parents' murders, stayed briefly in Jordan, and then found their way to the United States, eventually to an adoptive home in Ann Arbor. I contemplated the faces of those girls and the miracle of their safety, of their dancing, and I confronted the meaning of our reverse journey away from Ann Arbor to a region torn by violence.

I felt doubt. I felt a kind of shame at what I could afford to choose.

"Two roads diverged in a yellow wood."

I am living a life in which I am free to choose. It is without a doubt a harder and scarier life in Israel than in Ann Arbor. But the questions of how to be a person in the world—of how to recognize the suffering of others and do what one can to assuage it, of how to teach compassion and justice, of how to fight bigotry and racism, of how to limit violence, of how to vote and speak and write, of how to refuse to accept what should not be accepted, of how to assess personal risk and balance our fear with courage—these questions find us no matter where we live or where we try to hide.

And the language and culture in which we come to see these problems as our own define the range of possible answers. If I want my children and my children's children—if I myself want—to recognize and interpret these problems as contemporary Jews, steeped in the collective wisdom and textual inheritance of Jews, not alone but supported by the song and prayer of other practicing Jews, then Jerusalem is not a strange but a natural place in which to raise them. It is, then, an exquisite place in which to raise them.

I think back to Neruda and the land, the terrain Deshon called "the homeland":

"Pardon me, if when I want/To tell the story of my life/it's the land I talk about."

At a conference I go to in Jerusalem on Arabs and Jews sharing the homeland, a speaker quotes his rabbi and teacher as saying: "It is not that the land is ours. It is that we are the land's." The reversal is profound.

If the claims we feel upon ourselves are at times difficult to articulate or defend, they are no less real for that.

Where we serve, how we serve, what we have to offer: these are historical questions. In some ways, Smith School has brought me to Jerusalem.

◆　◆　◆

2013–2014—As my kids settle into Israeli life, I transport myself daily to America. In the garden outside our apartment, and often at the park down the block from Shai's *gan*, I sit while the kids are in school and read Diane Ravitch's *The Death and Life of the Great American School System*. Often, I buy a roll at the small shop across from the park, and although the flavorful bread tastes like Israel, I am in America's schools, so that when a woman turns to me, saying, "Good morning," in Hebrew, the language momentarily surprises me.

At night before bed, I read Sam Freedman's 1990 *Small Victories*, tracing the experience of a New York high school teacher in the classroom and beyond. An immersion story written by an accomplished education journalist, Freedman's book is the work of a writer who has gone into a school knowing precisely what he wants to do: observe, document, understand, and communicate to a broad audience the challenging realities of a school, a fine teacher, and her students. It is meticulous, detailed, and so compelling I often read late into the night, in spite of reading it on my computer screen. I also read the study by Freedman's student, Patrick McCloskey. In *The Street Stops Here*, he takes up the question of what private religious education can do in urban environments where students, particularly boys and young men, are often poised for failure.

These books are extraordinary. They evoke their worlds fully and make me hungry to learn more, even as it would also make sense for me to begin to inform myself about the Israeli school system. But Smith is still on my mind. I can't shake it.

One day a week, though, I set aside my books about America to read about the land of Israel and the State of Israel. On Wednesdays, I go to Elul, one of the first pluralistic centers for Jewish text study. Since it opened in 1989, it has sought the participation of secular as well as religious Jews in a country where there is less mixing between these groups than is commonly recognized. This year, the study group is comprised nearly entirely of native Israelis, and mostly Jerusalemites. It runs exclusively in Hebrew. We are about twenty: three young mothers, a number of retirees (a good many former school teachers), some professionals who devote one day a week to study, a few educators, a poet. They are wonderful people. It costs about six hundred dollars to participate for the year, and scholarships are available for those who need them.

This year, the theme of the study is "Here, on this land," a quote from the great national poet Rachel Bluwstein (1890–1931). While in most years, Elul devotes itself to a single text for study, this year we are alternating between two bodies of writing: the Mishnaic texts of Pe'ah (200–300 CE), the laws associated with the agricultural practices of leaving parts of one's fields for the poor, and the much later writings of the turn-of-the-twentieth-century Zionist thinkers who confronted the realities of building a state that would reflect Jewish ideals, as well as the various philosophical schools of their time. In addition to these texts, there is a third body: the personal stories that participants tell. These are stories of "here, on this land." Stories of parents and grandparents coming to this land, and staying on this land. These stories will stay with me.

Each week, the time is structured so that in the morning we sit in small learning circles (*havrutot*) of three or four, and read aloud and work through the knotty writings. In the winter, a small kerosene stove heats the room, and in the summer the fans whir. At mid-morning, we breakfast together, each week someone else responsible for the salads, cheeses, and breads, cakes, coffee, and tea. In the afternoon, we have time to respond to what we have learned in other forms: through photography, drawing, gardening, writing, the discussion of contemporary politics, and community action.

At day's end, together, we sing songs of the land of Israel, songs of yearning, love, suffering, and respite, and sometimes I find myself in tears, unaccountably. This group becomes a form of sustenance for me, especially in the harder days of being far from home and family, of supporting children in a foreign environment, and of wondering where we should live our lives.

Elul is housed in the homely bottom floor of an old apartment building in the German Colony, and one of the two group facilitators—Naama, the short-haired poet—has decorated the walls of the main study. Verses from the Torah and from the Talmud adorn the walls in ways that recall to me the many labels of Beit Rabban. Even more arresting are the large black and white photographs of some of the thinkers we are studying. Their long-ago eyes look into ours, and below their portraits Naama has placed the verse *v'hayu einekha ro'ot et morekha* (and your eyes shall see your teacher).

Your teacher: whoever he or she may be. In the verse from Isaiah, your teacher is God.

In this group, where there is no teacher, just two facilitators, we all sometimes teach and always learn. In this group, where many of us are or were once classroom teachers, we know the notion of "teacher" to be sacred but also broad, surprising in the way it eludes easy designation. We know it is not confined to the living or even to the once-embodied. Lovers of text, of memory and history, we know that books and voices can be among the great teachers of our lives.

I look again at the verse, its simple Hebrew words, and I try to see it as if I have never seen it before. I try to hear it.

Maybe the verse means that our eyes are always seeking teachers. Maybe it means that some of our teachers never depart from before our eyes. They become a kind of eyes for us. We attempt their sight. As a beloved teacher of mine once said, we ventriloquize their voices.

This is what the verse means to me as a student. When I listen to the verse as a teacher, I hear it differently, almost inversely.

The rhyme and the shared sounds of *roeh* and *moreh*—"to see" and "teacher"—suggest that sometimes the gift our teachers give us is the way they see us, or even simply *that* they see us. My eyes lift to see my teacher because my teacher is capable of seeing me.

It strikes me that the verse that hangs above the Ark in many synagogues applies here, too: "Know before whom you stand." Know, in the deep way that informs all you do. In the back-and-forth of sight, recognition, consciousness, is the possibility of transformation.

This is the work of religious life; it is also the work of teaching.

◆ ◆ ◆

One morning after the war, Shai asks me if I will please stay near his *gan*. He says it helps him to know I'm close. I have my laptop with me, and in a café down the block, I begin a new file. I begin to write about Smith: the kids, their responses to the poetry, the building, my drives to and from the school. The words come spilling out.

The next morning, Shai cries at the gate to the *gan*. He really doesn't want me to leave. His teacher pries him away and suggests that I go, quickly, and that he will get over it, as kids do. But Shai has not cried saying goodbye for years. Then the teacher calls me an hour and a half later, to tell me he is still crying. I am shocked that he has been crying for that long, and I am also shocked that she has waited this long to call me. I tell her I am coming to pick him up. She suggests that this is a bad idea, but I don't care. Enough pain for one day.

Walking home, Shai quickly calms down. We walk holding hands, and while I no longer carry him anywhere, he seems young to me in these moments, sweaty from tears and the heat of his tense body. He is not sick, he tells me, but worried. "How do I know you won't die?" he asks.

"Shai, love," I say, "you're right. All people die someday. But I don't have any reason to think Abba or I will die any time soon. We're healthy and young, and we try to be careful."

That does not soothe Shai, who is aware that people die from freak accidents, from unexpected missiles, and from cancers growing silently in their bodies. He is right, of course. The world is a very scary place—what we know of it and what we don't.

He wants to be near us all the time. When we are near, he seems like himself. But when we want to leave him places, even at a birthday party, he would rather leave with us and miss the party than be on his own.

A good friend gives us the number of a psychologist who works in both Israel and America and over the phone. He tells us that kids tap into this fear at different moments in their development and that Shai's sensitivity to some of the realities of Israeli life only exacerbates his natural fear. He tells us that it is not a great idea to leave him crying at the *gan* and count on him crying it out quickly, as a toddler might. He's not going to move on, not just yet. We need to show him we are with him before he will move on.

We go to see this psychologist in person and he tells us that he counsels parents to do what they can to support a child struggling through this by actually staying near him. I ask what parents do who work full time. He says, "Sometimes they set up a system where family members or friends alternate shifts at the child's school."

This all sounds exaggerated to me; I don't know anyone who has ever done this. And yet for two weeks, Shai cries every morning at the gate to the *gan*. We wind up walking back home with him some mornings. Other days, particularly if we need to be somewhere, we let him stay and cry, with me calling up to get reports that turn out to be either counterfactual, *hu b'seder gamur* (he is just fine), or optimistic, "he will be just fine." Our nonsystem is not working.

Ori and I decide to try the psychologist's plan. I talk to the teacher and tell her I want to sit in the *hatzer* (the playground area), so that Shai will know I am nearby. He will sit inside and do the things he is supposed to do, and I will sit outside. When he is ready, I will leave. She agrees, skeptically, to my American plan.

And so, I spend about six weeks in the shaded area of Shai's *hatzer*. The children come to know me and I learn their names. I remember that I am extremely comfortable in the company of children this age. I sit in a tiny chair or on the bench, with my laptop fully charged, on my actual lap, and I type.

I type without stopping. I type the story of Smith School and MSU, of America's haves and have-nots, of my own children and myself, of my dreams for schools and their realities.

I type Smith and MSU perched outside the kindergarten, with its photos of the prime minister and president hanging by the door, and its *mezuzah* on the doorpost.

I get up to stretch. I hear the children singing in Hebrew inside. I recognize that there is not a single Muslim child inside, nor any Christian children. I consider how politics is connected to my child's fear of my death. I wonder if there is any psychological state that is entirely independent of politics and I surmise that there is not.[8]

I feel extremely American, there in the *hatzer*, and at the same time, as my child becomes just a bit Israeli, learning the children's rhymes and songs that define generations to themselves, I imagine what it would be like to call this my home, to let go of the struggles of a faraway America and begin to fight here.

Teaching is a kind of fighting: the refusal to accept things as they are. I rarely think of it in these terms, but as I type Smith from Jerusalem, I become more interested in Jerusalem.

◆ ◆ ◆

Because I taught K-1 at Beit Rabban, my time there often comes to mind now that Shai is a kindergartener. I imagine what it would look like if Shai were there right now, in reading-writing workshop, morning explorations, community service. Sometimes when I pick him up on Wednesdays, I take him back with me to Elul, where I study, so that he can be in a "school" where learning is intimate. Naama, the short-haired poet, gives him crayons and paper. He draws while he listens to the adults around him learning and discussing. They are unstintingly kind to him, offering him chocolate and what is left of the day's cake. Sometimes he offers them drawings in return.

Meanwhile, I watch him taking it all in: the modest Israeli apartment space in which we learn; the voices, melodic in Hebrew; the particular mix of energy and peace that characterizes the rhythm of this learning; the black-and-white images staring forth from the walls. These moments between Shai and myself and what surrounds us are precious to me.

At his own school, Shai does not like his teacher. It is a shame because I know she is trying hard. She is new at the job and she is not especially creative. Her *gan* resembles hundreds of religious *ganim* in the city.

But Shai has come to Jerusalem from Ann Arbor. It is not an easy transplant.

"How can a teacher in a religious school yell so much?" he asks me.

He finds this a contradiction in terms. "It's like she doesn't understand she's religious," he tells me.

Having walked by many a district school and heard from outside the raised voices of teachers struggling for control, I doubt there are many kids in Jerusalem who associate religious Judaism with the absence of a teacher's shouting.

Other objections come up for Shai. They pray each morning at school. Praying itself is something Shai is very familiar with, from our synagogue and our home life. But now he is thinking somewhat differently.

"Yisrael, yisrael, yisrael," he says: we are always praying for ourselves, Israel or the Jews.

"What about *Adon Olam*?" Shai demands, referring to the prayer that declares God the master of the whole world.

"What about the people that aren't *Yisrael*?"—that aren't Jewish, he asks me.

This is a good question. Alone among his new friends, he seems to intuit that there must be children on the other side of Israeli wars. I tell him we pray for them, too. That we are both Jews and human beings.

But he's thinking all the time now, mulling.

This kind of mulling isn't new for Shai, but Israel brings it out in him, this tension of identity. He is not comfortable being part of the majority culture in a world he knows to be bigger. At six years old, he is already a child who was raised elsewhere. Or maybe he is a child who would have thought this way raised in our family, in any country. Or maybe he would have thought this way with or without us. In America, we have to remind him he is a Jew. In Israel, we have to remember we are human beings.

"I want to play soccer with Arab kids," he says, "but where can I meet them?"

How vividly this child of mine clarifies that there are no shortcuts, no simple places to raise children or to be adults. No schools that can rest easy. Or families. Or people. There is so much work to be done.[9]

◆ ◆ ◆

At times, I wonder how much that single class session about poverty and education brought me to Israel, via Smith, at this point in my life.

Later, I would revisit that session and recognize that what I had construed as callousness had been, in some cases, lack of knowledge or reflection. And I would know that Ori had been right to see it as a vital opportunity to challenge my students.

But at that moment, when my students had said things like, "Why should we care? These aren't our stories," all I could feel was an intense desire to be among people who shared my values. I had felt the desire to be "home," that is, to work among and for those to whom I was most primitively connected.

How complicated this thought-feeling is. It barely opens itself to analysis, even now, a few years later.

It was not that I thought Jewish students would not have said such things. Nor was I under the delusion that all Jews shared my feelings about race, money, education, or opportunity; I knew they did not. And conversely, I knew that people of other faiths or people of no religious faith at all might share many of my views.

Yet at that moment, in that classroom, I had never felt myself so much a Jew. And I did not feel at home.

For all my education in English literature and all my history in America, the words that jumped to mind there and then were Hebrew and ancient: *Pato'ah tiftah et yadkha l'ahikha* (You shall open your hand to your brother, your suffering, and your poor in your land).

There was no shortage of Jews who would not have applied such verses to the kids of Smith School. But for me they did apply. They were the language in which I thought about my responsibilities, most paradoxically, to the non-Jews who lived beside me, and lived in need.

Each of us has an origin. At that moment, my origin felt clear to me as it rarely did. I felt I was in the wrong place, working from the wrong base.

In the months that followed, that feeling eased. But it eased in a way that did not make me comfortable. It eased in a way that worried me.

I worried that, caught up in midlife, I had forgotten something.

When I was eighteen, I had not wanted to be American. I had wanted to be Israeli. I had seen myself first and foremost as a Jew. Later, at moments in my twenties, I had felt the pull to America more strongly. But then I had married and had children and made a career, and my home had been Jewish, while my work had been American.

At forty-three, I had spent my entire career in the American academy. I had taught texts of nineteenth-century slavery and abolition, English novels of the Industrial Revolution and the Woman Question, memoirs of the Holocaust, the history of literary criticism and theory, short fiction, epic, and poetry. Whether I was teaching in New York, Philadelphia, or Michigan, whether I was teaching texts that had originated on one side of the Atlantic or the other, my context was America. I read and taught twenty-first-century America because as much as texts are not mirrors in which to go seeking only ourselves, in the end, we read from the place we live. (As one of my teachers once put it, the texts we read read us.) And we can only be rooted in one place at a time.

Moving to Israel to teach English literature will mean teaching a new literature. Nothing will hold up intact, of that I am sure. I may teach from my old, well-worn novels, memoirs, and poetry, but I will be penciling new notes in the margins. Whether I am teaching Roethke or Hughes or Angelou, George Eliot or Virginia Woolf, I know what my challenging new subject will be: I will be studying what it means to teach the humanities to a mixed student body as a twenty-first-century Jew in a Jewish sovereign state. How great a shift in my interpretive base, in my teaching role.

In a tiny nation that is home to fewer universities than the state of Michigan, I will be part of a still tinier cadre of scholars and teachers devoted to the culture of letters. In a region maimed by war, misshapen by violence, fear, and prejudice, and defended from itself in ways I can only guess at, I know I will need to learn to teach again. What I bring with me from America will be foreign to my students, in spite of how familiar it will seem to me. I will live in a perpetual mix of the foreign and the familiar, and "home" will mean at first only my family and my books.

◆   ◆   ◆

I have lived in Israel for a full year now. From the vantage point of distance, but I think without nostalgia, I can see my great good fortune in having taught for ten years at James Madison College and four years at the University of Michigan, and having taught as a graduate student at my two alma maters, Barnard College and the University of Pennsylvania. It is clear to me every single day how fortunate I was to be trained as a teacher at Beit Rabban.

Many students I encountered in all those places have gone on to do important work in the world. In spite of the class session that so alienated me, I know that a great many of my students, particularly from James Madison College, have made career choices that ask them to sacrifice for the good of others and I am convinced that many of them do not feel it a sacrifice. They have learned to reflect, and perhaps even more important, they have found ways to translate their reflections from the sphere of analysis and thinking into actions that shape what Coles calls "morally courageous lives."[10] This does not mean heroic lives, but lives that respond to the moral implications of what one knows and sees of the world. Such lives entail the capacity not to deny but to look at reality, keep looking, and roll up one's sleeves: this may not be heroic, but it is something close, I think.

Kids I knew at Beit Rabban continue to flower. I was at one student's wedding a few months ago. She is now a social worker here in Jerusalem, treating survivors of sexual violence. She met her husband at a program that brings together Jewish Israelis with Palestinian activists. Another former student is now a doctor in England, specializing in infectious diseases and microbiology; a second works as a journalist in the United States; another is an expert on the debt ceiling and economic policy (a friend heard him on the radio the other day); and another studies the greenhouse effect from a lab in California. Yet another coordinates an organization that helps artists effect social change within the ordinary spaces of their communities. I am less interested in their pedigree—the outstanding universities they attended, the degrees they earned, their prestige or power—than in the kind of people they have become, the worlds they inhabit, and the roles they take in those worlds.

It is not hard to find the Kids of Beit Rabban of the 1990s. I can find most on Facebook, through mutual friends, or through their parents, many of whom live in the very same apartments as they did nearly twenty years ago, or at least in the same neighborhoods. Being a member of the educated middle class and above makes a person mappable; you leave a trace.

I have found two of the Smith kids on Facebook. Google turns up nothing on their names or any of their fellow students.[11] Maybe there is a different web that I can't find, on which they would be easily located; again, like Eula Biss's black news and white news, maybe I will never find them if I keep looking where I turn naturally. On the other hand, maybe they are still a little too young to be findable. In five years, I will know better.

I did a comparable search for my freshmen last year at MSU. They are also young, many with common names that would make it hard to distinguish them in a search, but I can find lots of them. Many of them have one accomplishment, perhaps in sports, that got them into a local paper in high school or they have signed up with "LinkedIn," which comes up on Google.

Some kids are findable, some are not. It's strange, but I find myself praying when I type in a Smith name on Google that it will come up, that we might live with a small measure of overlap in which we might seek each other out, read a poem together.

At Bar Ilan, I join a small group of colleagues in the Department of English. With one exception, my colleagues in English literature are all originally American or British, and were trained and taught in foreign universities before moving to Israel. Among us, we can count Yale, Harvard, Cornell, Columbia, Penn, Hopkins. At Bar Ilan, we are a small community among native Israelis and it is difficult not to compare even the physical challenges of teaching here to the comforts of teaching in some of America's better funded universities.

Coming from MSU, I have gone from a roomy office with five floor-to-ceiling bookcases, a swivel chair, a conference table, a desk, a wide window, and a Mac mini, with a departmental flatbed scanner and printer, to an office that resembles but falls short of a library study carrel. It is tiny, its curtains are literally torn, and its window is so dirty the whole world looks gray in spite of the sunshine. There is one short bookcase, an ancient desk, and one chair (where will a student sit?), and I am warned not to settle in because this office may not be mine more than one semester.

The bureaucracy is extremely difficult to manage; all university forms appear to need delivery in paper and in person, and then they get lost; the university is only slowly moving to electronic forms of communication. And while the librarian, a rare gem, could not be more lovely, the holdings in English literature are infinitesimal compared with those of any major American research university.

Yet my graduate students in creative writing are eager and rewarding. I am teaching one seminar in creative nonfiction, and there we build a family of twelve, reading and learning from the work of some of today's best English-language essayists. Meanwhile, the students work on their own essays. All are adults: two are retired from illustrious careers (in science and choreography); one is a young mother and a teacher; another is a psychologist; a few are full-time students; another is an arts therapist; another, a grant writer. People are writing on subjects ranging from what it has been like to live in Israel for decades as a German non-Jew, to having a father who suffers from multiple sclerosis, to growing up in New York with dyslexia before such diagnoses were readily available.

It is a pleasure to work with adults who want to write. They, too, feel the challenges of being immigrants and almost all are native English writers and speakers, so we can work beyond simple intelligibility toward craft and art.

It is in the undergraduate population that I find my teaching challenges. Although Bar Ilan is a religious university, my students are a mix of religious and secular, male and female, and most surprising, a nearly equal number of Jewish and Palestinian Israelis, all of whom see English as an important part of their future careers. These students come from across the country, since it is so small a land that commuting from even relatively far-flung cities and towns is possible. Many still live with their parents, though there are also students who room with others near the university. On the other hand, many students are already married and parents themselves, being part of populations who marry and bear children early, and also, in the case of the Jewish students, having served in the army and national service before beginning their college careers.

As I begin to work with these students, I am immediately brought up short by what, oddly, I did not anticipate: the marginality of high-level English discourse to contemporary Israeli life. This isn't a matter of the literature I teach, since George Eliot and Charles Dickens were as foreign and arcane to students in twenty-first-century Michigan as they are here. The marginality is a matter of language, the English language. Although my students have passed proficiency exams which qualify them for the English B.A. program, their writing nevertheless reveals it to be a secondary and still foreign language. I teach in English and I assign papers in English. And in my comments, I do much of what I did in the United States; I prod students to write clearly and succinctly, to argue their claims in thoughtful exploration of the texts they have read, to choose powerful and specific verbs, to avoid vague abstract nouns, and so on and so on. All this I do in English.

Yet English is not the language of public discourse. It is the primary language native Israelis want to know and master, because it is a language of power and opportunity, but it is not the language in which they debate the pressing affairs of the day or the language in which they contest a parking ticket, chat with other parents at the park, read the newspaper, or post in social media. Yes, the skills of analysis and argumentation are valuable in any language but the enormous effort it takes to foster such skills in non-native English makes me wonder if this is where my efforts are best applied. To the extent that any of these undergraduate students will write for readers, the great likelihood is that it will be in Hebrew or Arabic. When I worked with students at James Madison in Michigan, every ounce of energy I put into their English seemed a way of sowing seeds for the collective American future. Here, my love for finely written English may not be the best guide to the undergraduate classroom.

Teaching requires priorities and choices, often difficult choices to exclude or sideline certain aims, depending on the students in the classroom. Just as I had chosen at Smith School not to ask the students to *read* poetry, but to help them *hear* poetry, I think that the students at Bar Ilan may be better served if I focus my attention on their capacities for reading well, but even more, discussing well. The kind of nuanced and analytical reading and discussion that I cultivated in American college classrooms often seemed countercultural there. Here, it seems almost a dream from my past, rooted in another language and landscape. As threatened as the humanities often seem in the United States, they are even more so here in universities where the sciences and Jewish studies are the dominant fields. Meanwhile, the discourse community that I have consistently tried to build in my classrooms could not be more different than the norms of Israeli public discourse, where the art of listening is painfully underdeveloped and speech is often nothing but a contest of volume and force. I can see my opening here.

When the spring semester comes, I teach an introductory course called "Academic Writing 107." Of my fifteen students, I estimate that half are Jewish (some are from Russia, some are originally from the United States, and the rest were born in Israel) and half are Palestinian. Some of these latter live in the north of the country, while others live in its center. The names on the roster range from Tamar, Rachel, and Moshe, to Husam, Malak, and Heba. Many of the Arab students are female; like many of the Jewish female students, they dress to tell you something about who they are. Some come wearing a hijab while others are in jeans. Some write poetry or fiction in Arabic. Many want to be English teachers. Some are at Bar Ilan precisely because it is a religious university and so their families feel more confident that their own values will be upheld.

I am in a far more integrated classroom here in Israel than I ever experienced in the United States, as a student, teacher, or professor. I don't know what this new mix will bring. We will not be studying the Middle East. For now, we will not speak directly of our differences or our commonalities. But we will be in this room together twice a week for fifteen weeks, reading, writing, seeking understanding.

It will become a familiar space and the students will anticipate certain things when they enter. I will anticipate certain things when I enter. I suspect that English—both the language and the department, aloof in its way from the Hebrew-speaking, Israeli university—creates a kind of island for our students and for ourselves, their faculty. It is our version of a Little Italy, where the complicated national histories of English and American literature feel less critical than the chance to light the lamps, to find our missing siblings, to say our prayers, and remember our pasts. I do not minimize or romanticize the differences among our students, their opportunities and their histories, but I take English as a ground of possibility.

For so many years, Hebrew was my language of history and yearning, the sound-stream of dreams and fantasy, for myself and my children. Here in Israel, where my children chatter, sing radio jingles and pop singles, pray, read, and argue in Hebrew, I turn to English—for my children, for myself, for my students. In English, I reach for ideals and sensibilities that may not be fully realized in the America I know, but whose outlines are clear and recognizable. I turn to my bookshelves for myself, my children, my students, and I gather what seems right for each new day. The foreign and the familiar merge and emerge, their combination the weave of every English-Hebrew day.

In the months that come, in the muggy air of Ramat Gan, students will come in from corridors where they chat in Hebrew and Arabic to a class-room in which they will read in English. I will push them to read the full works, not the SparkNotes or the plot summaries which attract them, but the texts themselves, foreign and difficult, but worth the effort.

Together, we will read *A Christmas Carol* by Charles Dickens about the transformation of a life before it is too late. We will read *Silas Marner* by George Eliot about the transformation of *two* lives before it is too late. We will read "In Dreams Begin Responsibilities," by Delmore Schwartz, about whether it is always too late. And "Mother," by Grace Paley about it being certainly too late.

We will read the poem "Theme for English B," by Langston Hughes, and Jesmyn Ward's essays, *Men We Reaped*, on the deaths of five loved ones in Mississippi; we will marvel at how we do not give up trying to break from the plotlines history seems to have assigned us and we will witness the way speaking in the ringing, singular "I" remakes "we." We will read André Aciman's

"Shadow Cities" and wonder whether we can ever leave the places from which we come or transmit their truths to those who come from elsewhere. We will meet others in their lands, others in their lives and deaths.

I will want us to ask questions, to hear the questions being posed to us across time and space. I will tell the students about George Eliot and Charles Dickens, then about the worlds equally foreign to them that made Delmore Schwartz, Grace Paley, and Langston Hughes. To help them "see" the more recent American works, I will show them photos of Ward's region, the Gulf Coast after Hurricane Katrina, and Aciman's beloved Straus Park, the park I saw out my own window for three years at the turn of the twenty-first century. I know these photos mean entirely different things to me than they will to my students.

(My students. Already my students.)

But it is always this way. There is always a gap—between generations, between peoples and cultures, between teachers and students.

When I take attendance, I stumble over the names in Arabic; I know I am likely anglicizing the accents I cannot manage even after two or three tries. Meanwhile, the students struggle to address me, writing me e-mails that begin, "Hey my dear friend, Dr. Ilana." They write things like, "Professor Dr., will you be so kind to help me perfect my paper?"

The Jewish students clump together in one section of desks and the Arab students do the same, but I mix them up for writing exercises. I make sure they know each other's names. I see near-invisible shrugs and super-quick changes of expression; it is not all smooth sailing. Things are said aloud that make me tense, waiting for what will come next or what will remain silent and unsaid. But I also hear laughter as they share stories they have written in class. I see bodies slowly relaxing as the unknown becomes slightly more known.

We are not practiced at what we are doing. I am not yet practiced at much of what I am doing. But there *is* something we are doing together, some-thing we have agreed to, here in this dumpy classroom. What we are doing is a small, good thing. It sets up for other possible good things. I am not yet sure what they are but I am confident they exist.

The idea is to enter the classroom, day after day. And then, to exit—back out into the world. The door stays open.

◆   ◆   ◆

After my first full year at Bar Ilan, I return to our house in Ann Arbor to pack it up. The renters have gone and now we will put it up for sale. In packing,

I come across a large carton full to the brim with papers from Beit Rabban. Here is a red curriculum binder, and there, a blue spiral notebook full of lesson plans that only I can decipher; at the back are notes from an evening class I was attending at the time on the book of Exodus. Here are notes for a talk I gave to parents on invented spelling and emergent literacy in our classroom. Here are sentence strips, word trees in Hebrew, loose sheets with "Family Math" weekend activities, and stacks of articles that altered the way I would speak in classrooms for the two decades that followed and the way I would try to raise my children.

But most thrilling is the stack of student writing at the bottom of the box. I find mostly letters K-1 kids wrote to me in reading-writing workshop and stories that they gave me. I find a newspaper and a yearbook all in children's handwriting, and the letter written to the government representatives about homelessness. I find a word search a child made for me and a class book of fruits and vegetables from very early in the year, pictures labeled with single words. The construction paper is old now, and soft to the touch.

When I unearth these papers, I don't want to let them go. I pack them in my carry-on to take back with me to Jerusalem. And I think again of the wide spectrum from an excellent school to a failing school. I think of all that space in the middle.

In the middle are my children's current schools in Israel. If you ask me on most days, I would locate their schools smack in the middle. But right now, seeing these papers, transported back to the busy buzz of reading-writing workshop, back to the kids' immense energy to communicate and their avidity to listen, I reconsider. The middle is no longer the middle once you know what *can* be, once you have seen kids thriving in excellent schools. The middle is not really good enough. (And the not-good-enough to begin with are simply an absolute moral failure, unforgivable and impossible to redeem.)

In 2014 in Jerusalem, in a conversation with Devora about the schools in the middle, I say, "Parents tell me, 'We went to these schools and we came out fine.'"

She looks at me and says, "But what would fine-r look like?"

Suddenly "fine" has a different sound to it. Fine, in the now nearly obsolete sense of excellent, something to strive for, rather than "fine" in the sense of good enough, acceptable, passing. What we need are not fine schools, but finer schools.

◆   ◆   ◆

I am a mother, a university teacher, a Jew, an American, an Israeli, a twenty-first-century global citizen. I am a student and a reader and a writer. I may no longer own my own home, but I have a secure job, the certainty of food and shelter, the capacity, alongside my husband, to provide our children with much of what they need.

I ask myself, then, whose stories are my stories? Why should I care? About whom should I care? What would "finer" look like?

It is impossible to know what the future holds. But just as our hands record the passage of time, and sometimes testify to its ravages, so too can they write us into the future.

I hold my youngest daughter Tzipora's hand as she begins to form letters and our two hands write together.

These are the same hands with which we will give, and pray to receive.

DISCUSSION QUESTIONS BY THE AUTHOR

1. When you think of a "good education," what adjectives jump to mind? In chapter 1, Blumberg describes entering the classroom at Beit Rabban and feeling immediately that it is a place where she wants to teach. When you imagine a classroom that seems inviting and likely to foster a good education, what does it look like? How can the physical setup of a classroom speak to the values a teacher or school seeks to convey?

2. Think back to your own experiences as a student. What are some of the most memorable moments? What made them memorable? Were they moments you shared with other students? Was there a memorable moment when a teacher said something in the classroom or spoke to you privately? Were they connected to a particular discovery or a text? Consider writing about these moments and exploring them further.

3. If you or your children went to public school or if you teach in one, do you think of the school as raising its students to be American citizens? Global citizens? Why or why not? In what ways can a school educate its students toward greater universalism or greater particularism?

4. "Diversity" is often described as a primary American value. How much and what kinds of diversity did you encounter in your own education or in that of your children or students? When does diversity cease to be simply a demographic fact and become expressed in meaningful ways? (For example, in a math class? In the gym? In student council? In the school yearbook?) When does diversity pose genuine challenges or conflicts to mutual understanding? When do you feel it actively educates students? What, specifically, does it teach them?

5. Consider the possibility that the most significant form of difference in American society is economic. Is it important for children from different socioeconomic sectors to encounter each other? Is it important for them to go to school together?

6. In your own experience, what facets of American life are most segregated? Which are the least segregated? Can a homogenous neighborhood or

school use electronic or literary means to reach for more diversity or do such encounters need to occur in "real life"?

7. How and when should children from any socioeconomic sector be encouraged to move past their comfort zones and learn about or see social realities that differ from their own? When is genuine education uncomfortable? How can teachers be prepared for the emotional component that comes with new knowledge of the world?

8. How much do you think about the differences in American educational opportunity? Have you ever visited a school you weren't teaching in, studying in, or sending your children to? When you consider the span of social challenges facing your nation, is educational opportunity a primary one for you?

9. University teachers often encounter their students' resistance to new ideas, particularly ideas that are critical of a status quo or that hold up truisms to the light of inquiry. How might these resistances be addressed? How can a teacher encounter such resistance and allow its expression to enrich rather than shut down inquiry? Consider the role of memory and intellectual autobiography here. Do you think it is appropriate for teachers to share their own experiences of grappling with challenges to strongly held views? How might teachers dramatize their own lives of learning and development in ways that support their students' learning processes?

10. Do you think universities should have mandatory community engagement programs for all their undergraduate students? If you are connected to a university, do you see it as a social force in your town, city, state, or nation? Do you think it should be?

11. Early in the book, Blumberg describes a harmony of values she felt as an American Jewish child, but a conflict in her lived experience. Do you have another identity alongside your national one? Does it ever come into conflict with being American? Where does it work smoothly with your sense of being an American (or any other nationality)?

12. Blumberg questions the role literature plays in ethical development. What is the relation, she asks, in chapter 1, between "reading, empathy, and action"? Have any books made demands on you that you felt required action? Has any book changed your life? At what point in your life did you read it? Did you read it alone or in a social context? When

you think of reading now, do you imagine it as a solitary or a communal activity?

13. In chapter 3 and the postscript, Blumberg describes the challenge of finding schools in Israel whose values match her own. What are the dimensions of a school or classroom that are most important to you and that you would be unwilling to give up on?

14. Can you remember a time as a student when the messages you received at school differed sharply from the messages you received at home? Is it productive for a child to have to reconcile different messages from different authorities or do you think a child benefits from a unity of values in school and home (where possible)?

15. Think of the last assembly you went to at a school or a university. How did that assembly or ceremony convey the values of the institution? Were they values you share?

16. If you could continue your education right now, what would you want to study? When you consider your education, what was missing? What was most valuable?

17. If you were to tell the story of your education, what would be the critical episodes?

ACKNOWLEDGMENTS

My sincere thanks to those colleagues and friends who read sections or the entirety of the manuscript and improved it with their suggestions: Naomi Blumberg, Linda C. Dowling, Ariela Freedman, Jonathan Freedman, Sheila Jelen, Bill Kolbrener, Ilana Kurshan, Devora Steinmetz, and Haim Watzman. I am especially grateful to Devora Steinmetz for her careful readings of the manuscript and her immense assistance in delineating the dimensions of Beit Rabban that were most important to me to reconstruct here.

I would also like to thank the colleagues and friends who supported this project in other ways, across two continents: Karin Ahbel-Rappe, Zarena Aslami, Sandi Carothers, Evan Fallenberg, Sherman Garnett, Michael Kramer, Richard Primus, Yael Shapira, and Colleen Tremonte.

I gratefully acknowledge the students who gave me permission to reprint or describe their work here.

I am very grateful to the dedicated and keen readers for Rutgers University Press, and to Elisabeth Maselli and the diligent Press staff for their work on behalf of this book.

I am grateful to the whole of my extended family in the United States and Israel. Most of all, I thank Ori, Priya, Shai, and Tzipora. May our hands always be open to each other.

—Jerusalem, November 2017, Kislev 5778

NOTES

CHAPTER 1: LEARNING TO TEACH, TEACHING TO LEARN

1. For an excellent account of the narrative signs of fictionality and a powerful argument for maintaining distinct categories for historical and fictional narratives, see Dorrit Cohn, *The Distinction of Fiction*. On the particular cultural claims of autobiography, see Philippe Lejeune, *On Autobiography*.

2. For a condensed version of this episode, see Ilana M. Blumberg, "Traceable Beginnings: Reading and Writing Memoir in the Humanities Classroom."

3. The essay by Hayden White, "The Historical Text as Literary Artifact," provides a helpful synopsis of White's historiography. For a full discussion, see White, *Metahistory: The Historical Imagination in Nineteenth-Century Europe*.

4. Years later, I would investigate precisely this problem in George Eliot's work. See Ilana M. Blumberg, "'Love Yourself as Your Neighbor': The Limits of Altruism and the Ethics of Personal Benefit in *Adam Bede*."

5. The best introductions to the workshop approach are Lucy Calkins' two texts, *The Art of Teaching Writing* and *Lessons from a Child: On the Teaching and Learning of Writing*.

6. The educator Daniel Pekarsky has written an engaging and thorough account of Beit Rabban as a "vision-guided school." See Pekarsky, *Vision at Work: The Theory and Practice of Beit Rabban*.

7. John Dewey writes, "We may create in schools a projection in type of the society we should like to realize, and by forming minds in accord with it, gradually modify the larger and more recalcitrant features of adult society." *Democracy and Education*, 317. See also Devora Steinmetz, "School and Society: The Case of Beit Rabban."

8. See Calkins, *Lessons*, 47, where she discusses the consequences of drafting in classrooms where, "Most of the children approached a piece of writing knowing there would be a tomorrow."

9. Vivian Gornick offers an adept, nontechnical discussion of the narrating persona that is accessible to beginning students in her account, *The Situation and the Story: The Art of Personal Narrative*, which is a wonderful introduction to appreciating memoir.

10. For a discussion of ways to avoid a simplistic distinction between the narrated "I" and narrating "I," see Sidonie Smith and Julia Watson, *Reading Autobiography: A Guide for Reading Life Narratives*, 71–79. For the purposes of first-year students, however, the distinction is nonetheless a critical one.

11. George Eliot, *Middlemarch*, 129.

12. A manageable account that was instructive to me in those early years is Heidi Hayes Jacobs, ed., *Interdisciplinary Curriculum: Design and Implementation*.

13. Jacobs, *Interdisciplinary Curriculum*, 65.

14. https://www.loc.gov/rr/program/bib/ourdocs/Morrill.html.

15. My presentation was based on Nancy Sommers's article, "Revision Strategies of Student Writers and Experienced Adult Writers."

16. I give very little space here to this critical period of study in Israel and, in general, to my own Jewish education, because they are the subject of my book, *Houses of Study: A Jewish Woman among Books.*

17. Eliot, *Middlemarch,* 1.

18. Ibid., 23.

19. See Steinmetz, "School and Society," on the "presumption of sameness" undergirding most schools' educational approaches.

20. Suzanne Keen's study, *Empathy and the Novel,* has been an important text for me in my ongoing consideration of readerly identification, moral reflection, and action. See also my review of Keen in *Victorian Studies.*

21. George Eliot, "Review of the Natural History of German Life," (1856), in *Selected Essays, Poems and Other Writings,* 110.

22. Eliot, *Middlemarch,* 193.

23. Primo Levi, "On Obscure Writing," in *Other People's Trades.*

24. Jonathan Rosen, "The Trivialization of Tragedy," in *Best Contemporary Jewish Writing.*

25. In *Empathy and the Novel,* Keen argues, "Empathetic reading experiences that confirm the empathy-altruism theory . . . are exceptional, not routine" (65). She concludes this based on evidence drawn from neuroscientific findings, developmental and social psychology, and studies of affect and social cognition.

26. Robert Coles, *The Moral Life of Children,* 26.

27. Ibid., 26.

28. Ibid., 35.

29. Eliot, *Middlemarch,* 1.

30. In *Empathy and the Novel,* Keen writes, "The affirmation and challenge to convictions that can occur when readers discuss fiction, especially with the guidance of a teacher who connects the dots between reactions to fiction and options for action in the real world, can be considerable" (146).

31. Michael Higton, in *A Theology of Higher Education,* offers a Christian "theology of higher education," that succeeds, I think, in transcending a tradition-specific approach that would indoctrinate. He argues that universities should serve to promote "serious, socially inclusive, secular and religiously plural public arguments about the common good," shaping a spiritual discipline that is inherently social (8). Higton's argument suggests a viable historical and contemporary overlap between the civic mission of the university and a religious vision of the good: "education inherently takes the form of an interplay between wisdom and delight, in which wisdom seeks the flourishing of all God's creatures before God, while delight registers the distinctive way of being of all creatures called to share in this flourishing" (6).

32. See *The Cambridge Handbook of Service Learning and Community Engagement,* particularly the essay by Kristin E. Norris et al., "Critical Reflection and Civic Mindedness: Expanding Conceptualizations and Practices."

33. See Kwame Anthony Appiah, *The Honor Code: How Moral Revolutions Happen*, for his account of how honor works to make the previously thinkable unthinkable and vice versa in the moral lives of peoples.

34. I have described this project at more length in my essay, "Learning Chesed: Community Service in a Kindergarten Classroom." It is also represented in Pekarsky, *Vision at Work*, in his chapter on "Moral Education," 71–82.

35. Charles Dickens, *A Christmas Carol and Other Christmas Writings*, 39.

36. Stanley Cohen, *States of Denial: Knowing about Atrocities and Suffering*, 10–11.

37. Ibid., 9.

CHAPTER 2: CHOOSING TO LEARN, LEARNING TO CHOOSE

1. Anne Lamott, *Plan B: Further Thoughts on Faith*, 177–190.

CHAPTER 3: "IT'S THE LAND"

1. On recognizing the order and patterned structure within the apparent chaos of "toxic schools," see Bowen Paulle's study, *Toxic Schools: High-Poverty Education in New York and Amsterdam*.

2. Andrew Delbanco, *College: What It Was, Is, and Should Be*, 44.

3. Douglas Sloan, "The Teaching of Ethics in the American Undergraduate Curriculum, 1876–1976"; see particularly pp. 5–7. At times, the drive toward unity encouraged moral philosophers to actively avoid grounds of conflict, whether social or intellectual. Avoidance of the issue of slavery is a major example of this tendency (11).

4. Ibid., 11.

5. Lilian Katz, "Reading, Writing, Narcissism."

6. Eula Biss, "Black News."

POSTSCRIPT

1. See Matthew Lipman's insight about the essentially conservative nature of public schools: "If the school is looked upon as the representative of all social factions rather than of any one in particular, it is able to retain its claim to legitimacy in a democratic society, because it will not have surrendered its claim to impartiality. On the other hand, it will tend to be under these circumstances a very conservative—even traditionalist—institution." *Thinking in Education*, 10.

2. André Aciman, "Shadow Cities," in *False Papers: Essays on Exile and Memory*, 37–49.

3. I cannot stress enough the value of J. T. Dillon's findings in, "Using Questions to Foil Discussion." See also Dillon, "Student Questions and Individual Learning."

4. Dillon notes that when a student asks a genuine question, we can identify cognitive, affective, and behavioral dispositions in operation: the student experiences temporary

ignorance, perplexity, and the *need* to know. At the same time, the student is enacting dispositions of *desire* to know, *belief* in the presuppositions of the question, *faith* that an answer is attainable, and *courage* and *will* to pursue it ("Student Questions," 336). The form of genuine, pervasive inquiry that Dillon describes and that I attempt to evoke throughout this book is beautifully represented by bell hooks in *Teaching to Transgress: Education as the Practice of Freedom.* I see my own practice, which originates in Jewish faith, as similar to hooks' commitment to transformative education at all levels—to a radical, engaged pedagogy in a classroom community enmeshed in political reality.

5. See Dillon: "Practice everywhere designs to induce in students answers given by others to questions put by others. A complementary practice would invite student questions, forming their answers in the public light of joint inquiry" ("Student Questions," 341).

6. Ibid., 336.

7. It is now the case that a wide swath of American children feel themselves at great risk from school shootings. This sense was not nearly as widespread when I was composing the manuscript of this book.

8. Later, I encountered Robert Coles's claim that "a nation's politics becomes a child's everyday psychology." See Coles, *The Political Life of Children,* 310.

9. Stanley Cohen describes this as the "instinctive extensivity" of activists and people who identify more by virtue of common humanity than at the level of family, community, and country. He notes that at the sociological level, we don't know whether this state is fostered more by some political cultures than others. See Cohen, *States of Denial,* 265.

10. Robert Coles, *The Moral Life of Children,* 26.

11. Since finishing the writing of this manuscript, I have located one student, a particularly promising one, by mention in multiple state newspaper articles. He was arrested for a robbery at age eighteen, with two older men. He pled guilty, with terms that set his minimum prison sentence at forty-four months.

BIBLIOGRAPHY

Aciman, André. "Shadow Cities." In *False Papers: Essays on Exile and Memory*, 37–49. New York: Picador, 2001.

Andrews, Molly. *Narrative Imagination and Everyday Life*. Oxford: Oxford University Press, 2014.

Appiah, Kwame Anthony. *The Honor Code: How Moral Revolutions Happen*. New York: W. W. Norton, 2010.

Bartone, Elisa. *Peppe the Lamplighter*. Illustrations by Ted Lewin. New York: Lothrop, Lee and Shephard, 1993.

Biss, Eula. "Black News." In *Notes from No Man's Land: American Essays*, 75–88. St. Paul, MN: Graywolf, 2009.

Blumberg, Ilana M. *Houses of Study: A Jewish Woman among Books*. Lincoln: University of Nebraska Press, 2007.

———. "Learning Chesed: Community Service in a Kindergarten Classroom." *Kerem: Creative Explorations in Judaism* 3 (Fall 1995): 53–56.

———. "'Love Yourself as Your Neighbor': The Limits of Altruism and the Ethics of Personal Benefit in *Adam Bede*." *Victorian Literature and Culture* 37 (2009): 543–560.

———. Review of *Empathy and the Novel*, by Suzanne Keen. *Victorian Studies* 51, no. 2 (2009): 344–346.

———. "Traceable Beginnings: Reading and Writing Memoir in the Humanities Classroom." *Life Writing* 15, no. 1 (2016): 95–106. doi:10.1080/14484528.2016.1244469.

Calkins, Lucy. *The Art of Teaching Writing*. 1986. Portsmouth, NH: Heinemann, 1994.

———. *Lessons from a Child: On the Teaching and Learning of Writing*. Portsmouth, NH: Heinemann, 1983.

Cohen, Stanley. *States of Denial: Knowing about Atrocities and Suffering*. Malden, MA: Polity Press, 2001.

Cohn, Dorrit. *The Distinction of Fiction*. Baltimore: Johns Hopkins University Press, 2000.

Coles, Robert. *The Moral Life of Children*. New York: Atlantic Monthly Press, 1986.

———. *The Political Life of Children*. New York: Atlantic Monthly Press, 1986.

Delbanco, Andrew. *College: What It Was, Is, and Should Be*. Princeton: Princeton University Press, 2012.

Dewey, John. *Democracy and Education*. New York: Free Press, 1944.

Dickens, Charles. *A Christmas Carol and Other Christmas Writings*. 1843. Edited by Michael Slater. New York: Penguin Classics, 2003.

Dillon, J. T. "Student Questions and Individual Learning." *Educational Theory* 36, no. 4 (1986): 333–341.

———. "Using Questions to Foil Discussion." *Teaching and Teacher Education* 1, no. 2 (1985): 109–121.

Dolgon, Corey, Tania D. Mitchell, and Timothy K. Eatman, eds. *The Cambridge Handbook of Service Learning and Community Engagement*. Cambridge: Cambridge University Press, 2017.

Eakin, Paul John. *Living Autobiographically: How We Create Identity in Narrative*. Ithaca: Cornell University Press, 2008.

Eliot, George. *Middlemarch*. 1871–1872. New York: Bantam, 1985.

———. "Review of 'The Natural History of German Life.'" 1856. In *Selected Essays, Poems and Other Writings*, edited by A. S. Byatt and Nicholas Warren, 107–139. London: Penguin, 1990.

Fish, Stanley. *Save the World on Your Own Time*. New York: Oxford University Press, 2008.

Freedman, Samuel G. *Small Victories: The Real World of a Teacher, Her Students and Their High School*. New York: Harper Collins, 1991.

Gornick, Vivian. *The Situation and the Story: The Art of Personal Narrative*. New York: Farrar, Straus and Giroux, 2001.

Higton, Michael. *A Theology of Higher Education*. New York: Oxford University Press, 2012.

hooks, bell. *Teaching to Transgress: Education as the Practice of Freedom*. New York and London: Routledge, 1994.

Jacobs, Heidi Hayes, ed. *Interdisciplinary Curriculum: Design and Implementation*. Alexandria, VA: Association for Supervision and Curriculum Development, 1989.

Jensen, Meg, and Margaretta Jolly, eds. *We Shall Bear Witness: Life Narratives and Human Rights*. Madison: University of Wisconsin Press, 2014.

Katz, Lilian. "Reading, Writing, Narcissism." *New York Times*, July 15, 1993.

Keen, Suzanne. *Empathy and the Novel*. New York: Oxford University Press, 2007.

Kozol, Jonathan. *The Shame of the Nation: The Restoration of Apartheid Schooling in America*. New York: Random House, 2005.

Lamott, Anne. *Plan B: Further Thoughts on Faith*. New York: Riverhead, 2005.

Lejeune, Philippe. *On Autobiography*. Edited by Paul John Eakin. Translated by Katherine Leary. Minneapolis: University of Minnesota Press, 1989.

Levi, Primo. "On Obscure Writing." In *Other People's Trades*, 157–163. New York: Summit, 1989.

Lipman, Matthew. *Thinking in Education*. Cambridge: Cambridge University Press, 2003.

McCloskey, Patrick. *The Street Stops Here: A Year at a Catholic High School in Harlem*. Berkeley: University of California Press, 2010.

Michaels, Walter Benn. *The Trouble with Diversity: How We Learned to Love Identity and Ignore Inequality*. New York: Henry Holt, 2006.

Norris, Kristin E., et al. "Critical Reflection and Civic Mindedness: Expanding Conceptualizations and Practices." Dolgon 168–182.

Parker, David. *The Self in Moral Space: Life Narrative and the Good*. Ithaca: Cornell University Press, 2007.

Paulle, Bowen. *Toxic Schools: High-Poverty Education in New York and Amsterdam.* Chicago: University of Chicago Press, 2013.

Pekarsky, Daniel. *Vision at Work: The Theory and Practice of Beit Rabban.* New York: Jewish Theological Seminary of America, 2006.

Ravitch, Diane. *The Death and Life of the Great American School System: How Testing and Choice Are Undermining Education.* New York: Basic Books, 2011.

Rosen, Jonathan. "The Trivialization of Tragedy." In *Best Contemporary Jewish Writing,* edited by Michael Lerner, 230–240. San Francisco: Jossey-Bass, 2001.

Sloan, Douglas. "The Teaching of Ethics in the American Undergraduate Curriculum, 1876–1976." In *Ethics Teaching in Higher Education,* edited by Daniel Callahan and Sissela Bok, 1–60. New York: Plenum Press, 1980.

Smith, Sidonie, and Julia Watson. *Reading Autobiography: A Guide for Reading Life Narratives.* Minneapolis: University of Minnesota Press, 2001.

Sommers, Nancy. "Revision Strategies of Student Writers and Experienced Adult Writers." *College Composition and Communication* 31, no. 4 (December 1980): 378–388.

Steinmetz, Devora. "School and Society: The Case of Beit Rabban." https://www.academia.edu/6121067.

Swofford, Anthony. *Jarhead: A Marine's Chronicle of the Gulf War and Other Battles.* New York: Scribner, 2003.

Tough, Paul. *How Children Succeed: Grit, Curiosity, and the Hidden Power of Character.* New York: Houghton Mifflin, 2012.

White, Hayden. "The Historical Text as Literary Artifact." In *Tropics of Discourse: Essays in Cultural Criticism,* 81–100. Baltimore: Johns Hopkins University Press, 1986.

———. *Metahistory: The Historical Imagination in Nineteenth-Century Europe.* 1973. Baltimore: Johns Hopkins University Press, 2014.

ABOUT THE AUTHOR

ILANA BLUMBERG is director of the Shaindy Rudoff Graduate Program in Creative Writing at Bar Ilan University and senior lecturer in English Literature. She taught at Michigan State University for ten years, as associate professor of humanities at James Madison College, and was a founding teacher at the Beit Rabban Center for Education in New York City. Blumberg is the author of the prize-winning memoir *Houses of Study: A Jewish Woman among Books* (University of Nebraska Press, 2007), and *Victorian Sacrifice: Ethics and Economics in Mid-Century Novels* (Ohio State University Press, 2013). She has won teaching awards from the University of Pennsylvania and Michigan State University.